THE STUARTS IN 100 FACTS

ANDREA ZUVICH

AMBERLEY

Dedicated to my dear mother, Edelmira Guadalupe Muñoz Sepulveda.

First published 2015

Amberley Publishing
The Hill, Stroud
Gloucestershire, GL5 4EP

www.amberley-books.com

British Library Cataloguing in Publication Data.
A catalogue record for this book is available from the British Library.

ISBN 978 1 4456 4730 2 (paperback)
ISBN 978 1 4456 4731 9 (ebook)

Typeset in 11pt on 13.5pt Sabon.
Typesetting and Origination by Amberley Publishing.
Printed in the UK.

The Facts

Introduction

The Stuart Era officially spanned the years from 1603 to 1714, and was a truly unique period in history. It was also an extremely volatile one, which saw the violent clashing of superstitious medieval beliefs with the reason and ideals of the Enlightenment. Although it is largely a neglected period in terms of popularity when compared with the Tudors, for example, there is no justification for such indifference. The Stuart period is simply too full of action, adventure, passion, chaos, violence, beauty, tragedy and monumental changes to the socio-political pattern of the United Kingdom to be ignored. At times, the moral pendulum swung from strict puritanism to full-on hedonism. I have been fortunate to be able to devote many years of my life to the study of the Stuart period – a part of history that I find utterly mesmerising.

Needless to say, to condense the near-endless number of facts about this period into just 100 was no simple task, for there are many fascinating topics that have had to be set aside. Please note that these facts are not meant to be in-depth academic analyses of the events or people of the time, but rather a taste of what this era has to offer. Hopefully, readers will be inclined to seek out more books about the subjects and topics discussed herein. The Stuart Era was not just about moody-faced Puritans dressed in black (as popular culture may have us think), but about events and ideas that ultimately shaped the modern world in which we live. I hope you enjoy the facts that I have selected, and that they may tempt you to learn more about this fascinating era in history.

1. The End of the Tudors Was the Start of the Stuarts

On 24 March 1603, the last of the Tudors breathed her last. Queen Elizabeth, the daughter of King Henry VIII and his second wife, Anne Boleyn, had enjoyed one of the most successful reigns in English history. The Tudors had reigned since Henry Tudor defeated King Richard III at the Battle of Bosworth Field in 1485, and had presided over monumental changes to the religious fabric of the nation. Elizabeth's father controversially broke from the Roman Catholic Church and established himself as the Supreme Head of the Church of England – thereby creating the Anglican Church. When Elizabeth's elder half-sister, the Catholic Queen Mary I, died in 1558, Elizabeth began a reign that lasted for nearly forty-five years. Under her, Drake and his sea-dogs had defeated the powerful Spanish Armada, and literature and the arts flourished in a Golden Age.

There was just one problem. Although there were many suitors for her hand, Elizabeth never married, and thus had no heir. Even as she lay dying upon the cushions spread out under her in her chamber in the Palace of Richmond, there was uncertainty as to who would next sit upon the throne of England. There were rumours that James VI of Scotland would be named heir, for James was a member of the Scottish royal family, the Stewarts – who are usually referred to by the Gallicised spelling of their surname, *Stuarts*. (There is no 'correct' spelling, as both are accepted, but the latter is the one most used by historians.) James's mother was none other than Mary, Queen of Scots, who had been executed in 1587 under Elizabeth's reluctant orders. Scotland and France had many ties; Mary was once a Queen of France, and her mother, Mary of Guise, was a French princess. The rumours proved to be true, and the throne of England passed to the King of Scotland, making him King James I of England.

But Elizabeth, splendid queen that she was, had nevertheless left her successors several problems, including a potential powder-keg of religious sectarianism. Catholics, once the majority before the upheaval of the English Reformation, were marginalised, while the more extremist fringes of the Protestants weren't content with Elizabeth's policies. One of the criticisms sometimes placed at Elizabeth's door is that she didn't think in the long-term, or about the potential issues with which her successors would have to contend. King James I had to tread carefully; and, by and large, he did.

In all, there were seven Stuart monarchs, and two Lords Protector, that followed Elizabeth to the throne: James I, ruled 1603–25; Charles I, ruled 1625–49 (executed); Interregnum/Commonwealth of England (1649–60), during which time Oliver Cromwell was the Lord Protector (1653–8), followed by his son, Richard, Lord Protector from 1658–9; Charles II, ruled 1660–1685; James II, ruled 1685–8 (exiled); William and Mary, ruled 1689–94 (Mary's death); William III, ruled alone, 1695–1702; and Anne, ruled 1702–14. Elizabeth's legacy was so great that James I's great-granddaughters Mary II and Anne would eventually be favourably compared with the Virgin Queen – although neither would ever truly fit her shoes.

2. There Were Two Calendars in Use

One of the most important things to understand about Stuart-era history is that there were two calendars in use in Europe at that time. Are you confused? Don't worry – that's a completely normal response at first. The calendar most people use nowadays is the Gregorian calendar. The United Kingdom has been officially using this calendar since the eighteenth century (1752, to be precise), but in the seventeenth century, several countries – including England – still used the ancient Julian calendar. Scotland was ahead of the game, though, for they had adopted the new Gregorian calendar back in 1600.

The Julian calendar that everyone knew and loved was named after Julius Caesar, who is credited with having reformed the Roman calendar to be more accurate. Yes, that's the same Julius Caesar who conquered Gaul, had an infamous affair with Cleopatra, and was stabbed to death on 15 March in 44 BC. Now, historians often refer to the Julian calendar as the Old Style or O.S. calendar. The Gregorian calendar is therefore the New Style or N.S. calendar. This calendar was introduced under Pope Gregory XIII in 1582. Of course, given that a Catholic introduced this calendar, Protestants (who were on the rise in Europe) were sceptical – some thought it was a Catholic plot – and this is one of the reasons why the Gregorian calendar took quite a while to get accepted. Most of the Catholic countries – France, Spain, Portugal, Italy, and Poland – had adopted the Gregorian calendar quickly in the late sixteenth century.

If you visit St George's Chapel in Windsor Castle in Windsor, England, you'll see that the ledger stone upon which Charles I's death date is engraved states that he died in 1648. This is correct, according to the Old Style calendar. Most historians now say he died in 1649, because that corresponds to the correct year in our calendar – the Gregorian/New Style calendar. The Julian/Old Style calendar's New Year fell upon 24 March, not 1 January, so when Charles was executed on 30 January 1649, it was still 1648 *in England*.

In the seventeenth century, the calendars were different by ten days. For example, when Prince William III of Orange married Mary Stuart at St James's Palace, England, on 4 November 1677, it was technically his birthday as well, since back home in the Dutch Republic (where the Gregorian calendar was already in use) it was 14 November. Things got a bit trickier with the dawn of the eighteenth century when, in 1701, the difference between calendars moved from ten days to eleven days. The reason behind this was that when the Gregorian calendar was created, it took into account the fact that the Julian calendar was inaccurate, becoming even more so every 100 years. Accordingly, in 1582, ten days were removed in order to make the new calendar accurate. Fast forward to the adoption of the Gregorian Calendar in 1752, and 11 days were added to catch up. One plus side – if things don't go well in January you can always 'start over' again in March.

3. Flirty Minette Had a Sad Time of It ... as Did Her Daughters

Princess Henrietta Anne, affectionately known as 'Minette', was the youngest child of Charles I and his wife, Henrietta Maria. Born in Exeter during the English Civil War on 16 June 1644, the young princess's childhood had little stability. Two years later, she was smuggled out of the country and brought up at the French court, where she eventually married Philippe, duc d'Orléans – the younger brother of King Louis XIV. Philippe was what we would today define as homosexual. Unfortunately, his behaviour left much to be desired; he was intensely jealous, petulant and arrogant. 'Monsieur', as he was known, cruelly carried on his affair with the Chevalier de Lorraine right in front of his wife, who was known as 'Madame'. Minette was an ebullient and attractive young woman, and her great popularity simultaneously made Monsieur jealous and envious. Minette appears to have had a brief fling with her brother-in-law, Louis XIV, but that died down quickly and he was soon in an affair with her lady-in-waiting, Louise de La Vallière.

'Madame' was the means by which her brother, Charles II, agreed to the secret Treaty of Dover with Louis XIV. While she was in England with her family, she had a largely happy time of it and Louis even allowed her to stay longer, in spite of his brother's demands that she return home. Shortly after returning home to France, however, the twenty-six-year-old Minette suddenly became violently ill and died at the Château de Saint-Cloud. Rumours swept the courts that she had been poisoned. For a while, even Charles appears to have believed this to be the case, because 'Monsieur' and his close associates had treated Minette appallingly – so it sadly wouldn't have been much of a surprise if they had indeed poisoned her. Most historians, however, believe that Minette may have suffered from anorexia and that her death was probably due to acute peritonitis.

Minette's eldest daughter, Marie Louise (1662–89), fared little better. Marie Louise was married to King Carlos II of Spain, the last Hapsburg, who was a sad product of generations of close inbreeding. The king's unfortunate lineage produced in him a vast array of debilitating physical and mental disabilities. Although Carlos loved his wife, and she seems to have returned his affections, they were unable to have children (he was, in all likelihood, impotent). Marie Louise, depressed and lonely, died under mysterious circumstances, leading to rumours that she had been poisoned – like mother, like daughter.

Anne Marie d'Orléans (1669–1728), Minette's youngest daughter, had the least tragic life out of the three ladies, although it was still unhappy. She was married off to Victor Amadeus II of Sardinia, whose infamously obsessive affair with Jeanne Baptiste d'Albert de Luynes she was forced to endure. Anne Marie got the last laugh, though, for her grandson became King Louis XV of France.

4. The Bills of Mortality Included Some Truly Horrific Causes of Death

Death by intestinal worms, anyone? While most people, according to the figures listed in the *Bills of Mortality*, died from such common ailments as 'childbed', 'ague' and 'fever', there were some that can only be described as horrific. So what were the *Bills of Mortality*? These papers were statistics published weekly about the causes of death (mortality) for that week, and as such are a great resource. That being said, diagnosis during the Stuart age was not very specific, so those listed under one disease probably had another. We have to keep in mind that life for most people was quite insalubrious. There was little notion of infection control, germs or basic hygiene.

Those who died suffering from mental disorders were under 'Lunatick and frenzy'. Suicides are also mentioned, for they 'hanged and made away 'emselves'. A look at the week of 20–27 September 1670 indicates the usual suspects: 'Aged' – or elderly – with twenty-four deaths, 'Consumption' or tuberculosis with sixty-four deaths, but the cause of the most deaths that week was 'Griping in the guts', with a whopping 150 deaths. 'Egad! What is that?' you may well ask. Think about the worst upset stomach you've ever had, plus violent diarrhoea, and you get an idea of what this was like.

Parasites were an unfortunate aspect of daily life in Stuart Britain, and many people suffered and died from typhus and plague – and then there were the worms. Intestinal worms were parasites that would lay eggs in the intestines and eat the nutrients from the food a person ate, but then they'd also begin eating away the intestines too. This was awful, and physicians later gave patients potentially dangerous remedies, which contained toxic substances, to combat it. Intestinal worms are still a problem, but they can now be killed with a dose of the drug *mebendazole.* The 'Bloody flux' was another intestinal affliction most commonly believed to be a form of dysentery, which involved frequent and bloody diarrhoea.

Malaria, which is usually contracted from a mosquito bite, crops up in the *Bills of Mortality* as well. In the European Malaria Epidemic of 1678–82, thousands of people became infected with the disease; it made its victims feverish, fatigued, and sweaty, but it could also kill. Over a thousand people died of this malarial fever in the autumn of 1680 alone. Even royals were not immune: Charles II contracted it and his niece, Mary, Princess of Orange, often suffered from malarial 'agues'.

Lifestyles and their accompanying diseases have changed rather considerably since the Stuart period. On the one hand, people in wealthier nations are living a good deal longer than their Stuart-era ancestors and aren't dying from worms, plague, dysentery or griping in the guts. On the other, most of the *Bills of Mortality* indicate very low numbers of deaths for cancer and diabetes compared to our time now. According to the WHO, cancer, cardiovascular diseases and diabetes account for the most of the deaths today among those who live in higher-income societies.

5. The Coffeehouse Was the Place to Be

Coffee is unquestionably one of the most popular beverages in the world. During the Stuart era, coffee was one of a bevy of exotic foods and beverages that came into Britain – and it certainly caused a stir. Alcoholic beverages imbibed in taverns and alehouses were still extremely popular, but the new coffee drink could be enjoyed without a hangover and so it became popular with the intellectuals of the day. That being said, some people mixed liquor into their coffee. Coffee wasn't the only hot beverage consumed in a coffeehouse, for coffee's equally exotic cousins, hot chocolate and tea, were also served.

These establishments were also places in which men could smoke (this custom famously being brought over from the New World by Sir Walter Raleigh during Elizabeth's reign), and so the interiors of coffeehouses would be smoky as men smoked the tobacco from their long clay pipes. Stuart-era scientist Robert Hooke enjoyed partaking of a coffee and a smoke in his favourite coffee house, Jonathan's, in Exchange Alley. Coffeehouses popped up all over town, including Will's, Lloyd's, Garaway's, Man's (Wren's favourite) and The Grecian, among others.

Coffeehouses were not just places in which one could relax or discuss intellectual matters; they were also the perfect locations for business. Auctions took place in these establishments as well. The aforementioned Lloyd's Coffee House on Tower Street in the City of London was owned by Edward Lloyd and became important in the world of finance and insurance, for it was here that *Lloyd's of London* – one of the major specialist markets – was founded. The latest newspapers would be on the tables and men could discuss politics and even exchange gossip.

Political discussions could lead into political dissent and so coffeehouses began to be seen as dangerous establishments – nests of sedition and intrigue. This can clearly be seen when Charles II decided to close coffeehouses. On 29 December 1675, the king issued a *Proclamation for the Suppression of Coffee-Houses*, stating that they 'have produced very evil and dangerous effects'. Unsurprisingly, the backlash was huge. The Eighteenth-century historian and philosopher David Hume wrote, 'The king, therefore, observing the people to be much dissatisfied, yielded to a petition of the coffee-men, who promised for the future to restrain all seditious discourse in their houses.' As a result, Charles had the proclamation recalled.

That being said, the king was not the only one annoyed by the allure of the coffeehouses. In 1674, wives joined up and published *The Women's Petition Against Coffee!* In this, they claimed that coffee – an 'abominable, heathenish liquor' – made their husbands impotent, among other things. Why didn't these ladies simply join their husbands for a cup or two? Women generally were not allowed in coffeehouses unless they worked there, and in sketches and drawings from the time, there is usually a woman behind the counter – the customers are all men. Women were more likely to go into the various eating-rooms that could be found. Eventually, coffeehouses evolved into gentlemen's clubs.

6. John Aubrey Wasn't Very Good at Completing His Projects

We all know someone who starts a project with great enthusiasm only to end up never completing it. Whether due to procrastination, an interminable drive for perfection, or merely a loss of interest, John Aubrey (born in 1625/6) was not very good at completing his projects. Take for example his most famous work, *Brief Lives*, which is a series of mini biographies of important people that lived in his lifetime or before. It makes for a fascinating and slightly gossipy read, but for the fact it was never truly completed – and the *Brief Lives* we can read today has been meticulously edited and compiled by other people over the three centuries since his death.

Aubrey's other works were also unfinished and needed helping hands to sort them out for publication. *Miscellanies Upon Various Subjects* was begun by Aubrey in 1652 and he kept working on it, off and on, until the 1690s. At that point he sent it to James, Earl of Abingdon, and wrote, 'It was my intention to have finished my Description of Wiltshire (half finished already) ... but my age is now far too spent for such undertakings.' Accordingly,he gave the task of completing it to a certain Thomas Tanner. Aubrey died in 1697. Whatever the reasons were for his seeming inability to complete his projects, his passion and devotion to keeping a record of historical people are commendable – and the bits of his work that is available are certainly enjoyable and enlightening.

7. George Villiers Enjoyed a Meteoric Rise to Power, but a Vile End

George Villiers had it all: incredibly good looks, intelligence, charisma, and the most powerful benefactor in the country – the king. James I (VI of Scotland) was a rather odd fellow, whose court was considered debauched in comparison with that of his predecessor. While very learned, the king had a proclivity for being quite coarse and vulgar at times. He had several male favourites (who were rumoured to have been his lovers) including Robert Carr (or Kerr), Earl of Somerset, and George Villiers. It was the latter, Villiers, who has become considered as the most important of James's favourites.

King James and George Villiers had a very affectionate correspondence, in which the latter was referred to as 'Steenie' (after the beautiful St Stephen) and also referred to as his 'sweet child and wife'. Villiers, in turn, called James 'Dad'. James heaped honours and titles onto his handsome young favourite – including making him the 1st Duke of Buckingham. Villiers' meteoric rise to fame and fortune made him both fiercely hated and loved. Buckingham and James referred to Prince Charles, who would later become the ill-fated Charles I, as 'Baby Charles'. After initially disliking Buckingham, Charles ended up with a strong admiration for him. Buckingham seduced and married the very wealthy heiress, Katherine Manners, which made for a great scandal at the time. George had several lovers, including Lucy Hay, Countess of Carlisle, and there were even rumours that he was romantically involved with Queen Anne of France.

When James died and Charles became king on the

27 March 1625, George's position was stronger than ever because the new king depended upon him greatly. When Charles married the French princess Henrietta Maria later that year, she detested her husband's favourite. One can only be on the top for so long, and in 1628 George Villiers soon came to a sticky end when he stayed in the Greyhound Inn in Portsmouth. There, John Felton, a disgruntled seaman who had come to blame Buckingham for his troubles, stabbed the thirty-five-year-old to death. Buckingham's assassination was met with widespread approval, as he had been almost universally despised for some time. Many had come to see him not only as completely incompetent in both the political and military arenas, but also plain wicked.

Charles gave his dear friend a splendid state funeral, but the route was lined with hostile persons who spat towards the coffin as it went by. Felton paid for his (rather popular) crime by hanging from the Tyburn tree two months later, in late November 1628. Even Henrietta Maria, who for much of her early marriage was in Buckingham's shadow, was pleased with one notable outcome of his demise: husband and wife grew closer and they embarked upon a much happier relationship.

George Villiers, 1st Duke of Buckingham's legacy has been assured, thanks to the historical fiction literature of the nineteenth century – he is best known now as a key figure in Alexandre Dumas's *The Three Musketeers*.

8. Charles II Couldn't Keep It in His Pants

One of the tawdriest facts about the Stuarts is that several of them were highly sexed, and perhaps none more so than Charles II – who didn't seem able to keep it in his pants. His many romantic, and later adulterous, liaisons are the most popular subject about him and unfortunately tend to overshadow the various political events of his reign. Unlike his father, Charles I, the second Charles proved to be a blatant, serial womaniser who had thirteen illegitimate children (that we know of!) and more mistresses than we could say. Charles II is not known as 'the Merry Monarch' for nothing …

Lucy Walter, the attractive Welsh Royalist exile, was Charles's first major mistress. In April 1649, she bore him his eldest and most beloved son, 'Jemmy', James Crofts, later James Scott, Duke of Monmouth. After Charles's ardour had cooled, Jemmy was taken from his mother and Lucy eventually died in poverty.

Next came the volatile Barbara Palmer, née Villiers, who was as calculating and domineering as she was beautiful and fecund (she gave birth to five children with Charles). Barbara was capable of some major scenes of histrionics when she didn't get her way and Charles eventually got fed up with her behaviour.

'Pretty, witty Nell', as described by Samuel Pepys, is by far the most popular of all of Charles II's many mistresses. Her rise from impoverished orange-seller to popular actress to king's mistress was no mean feat. Nell gave her lover more children, sought and obtained the freehold on her London property and also owned Burford House in Windsor.

Nell's contemporary rival was Louise de Kerouaille, whom Charles referred to affectionately as 'Fubbs' because she was a little chubby. As popular as Nell was, Louise was reviled, because she was French and Catholic – two things that were quite unpopular in Stuart England at the time. Charles bestowed upon his French mistress the title of Duchess of Portsmouth.

Both Nell and Louise were sidelined when Italian beauty Hortense Mancini arrived on the scene. Hortense was one of the gaggle of Cardinal Mazarin's nieces who were popularly referred to as The Mazarinettes. Hortense was a promiscuous, pleasure-loving, whirlwind of a woman, and liked to push the envelope. Unfortunately, she pushed things way too far when she began an affair with one of Charles's daughters, Anne. She may have also had a relationship with the female Restoration playwright Aphra Behn.

Charles also bedded the actress Moll Davis, who unfortunately fell foul of one of Nell's jokes. Nell gave her food laced with a strong laxative and when Charles came for his assignation with her she was rather under the weather! Despite his obvious inability (or refusal) to be faithful, Charles seemed to be fond of his wife, Catherine of Braganza. Although he had been under great pressure to divorce her from his ministers in order to have legitimate children with another, he never did. He must have (dare we say it?) loved Catherine, in his own way.

9. Mathematical Genius Isaac Newton Thwarted a Counterfeiter

Isaac Newton, Fellow of the Royal Society, is remembered in history as one of the greatest scientists who ever lived. Newton, the genius behind the theory of gravity and the author of scientific works *Principia Mathematica* and *The Opticks*, was a Cambridge professor who thrived on intellectual discussion and alchemical experimentation. Although he had an inauspicious birth in Lincolnshire in 1642, he did very well in his studies and became a major early figure in the Enlightenment due to his many scientific achievements. He was known for being exacting and was often getting into arguments with fellow scientists such as Robert Hooke and John Flamsteed, among others.

It may come as a surprise that this great man of mathematics and science was called upon to put a stop to counterfeit money, but that's precisely what happened in the 1690s. Counterfeiting was a major problem during this time, and Charles Montague, who was Chancellor of the Exchequer at the time, believed that Newton was the best person to sort it all out. The currency was devalued and many coins were clipped, meaning people cut slivers off coins from around the sides, and these clippings were melted down and mixed with inferior metals; the whole circumstance was severely devaluing the nation's currency.

And so in 1696, Newton became a Warden at the Royal Mint (which was then based in the Tower of London), and this is where he oversaw the production of new, state-of-the-art coins. On 2 May 1696, Newton had to take an oath before three Lords of the Treasury that he would not 'reveal or discover to any person or persons whatsoever, the new invention of rounding the money and making the edges of them with letters or grainings'. In other words, he had to keep everything a secret. In 1698, Newton oversaw the Great Recoinage, wherein coin money was created in such a way as to prevent currency clipping. This is why we have ridges and designs on the sides of coins.

According to *Newton and the Counterfeiter* author Thomas Levenson, William Chaloner was a very successful counterfeiter who produced £30,000 of counterfeit money. Chaloner was a tricky devil because he was intelligent and ruthless. His nasty streak included going around to printers and trying to see which ones would print his phony Jacobite pamphlets. He informed on those who agreed to print them and these printers were sentenced to death. Once Newton was on Chaloner's trail, however, the counterfeiter's days were numbered. After some cat-and-mouse chasing, Newton finally caught Chaloner. On 3 March 1699, Chaloner was found guilty and sentenced to death by hanging. The sentence was carried out on 22 March 1699. Newton, now a hero, was given the position of the Master of the Royal Mint – one he would keep until his death in 1727.

Next time you think about Isaac Newton, remember that he was not only a mathematical genius ... he was a crime fighter!

10. Guy Fawkes Was Neither an Anarchist Nor the Ringleader of the Gunpowder Plot

5 November, commonly known as Guy Fawkes Day, celebrates the thwarting of the plot to blow up Parliament, which would have assassinated James I and leading politicians in attendance. Modern popular culture has turned Guy Fawkes into a major figurehead for anarchy and left-wing politics. The real Guy couldn't have been more different. Fawkes, like the rest of the plotters, was in fact a very conservative Catholic, who was deeply unhappy with how Catholics were being persecuted. Before the massive upheaval of the English Reformation and the Dissolution of the Monasteries, begun during the reign of Henry VIII, England had been a predominantly Catholic country. Henry VIII broke from the Catholic Church and established himself as the Head of the Church of England. The plotters didn't want anarchy, but to bring the country back to what it had been – Catholic – or at least to be able to worship freely.

When everyone gets caught up in talking about Guy Fawkes, they tend to forget about one very important detail: he was just a minor figure. The leader of the Gunpowder Plot was actually Sir Robert Catesby, whose family, like many others, had become disenfranchised under the harsh anti-Catholic laws. Catesby had several other co-conspirators: Thomas Percy, Francis Tresham, John Wright, Christopher Wright, Thomas Winter, Robert Winter, Ambrose Rookwood, Sir Everard Digby, Robert Keyes, John Grant, and Guido Fawkes. They didn't even want to abolish the monarchy, but instead to install James's daughter Elizabeth as a Catholic queen (her elder brother Henry would probably be killed in the blast). The vaults which lay beneath the chamber were available to rent and the conspirators rented the space and began filling it with thirty-six barrels of gunpowder (hence the 'Gunpowder Plot').

Needless to say, things didn't go according to plan. Tresham's brother-in-law, Lord Monteagle, received a letter (probably sent by Tresham) warning him not to go to Parliament that day for 'they shall receive a terrible blow. Alerted by the tip-off, guards went down to the vaults and had a look around. There, they found Fawkes right beside many barrels of gunpowder.

When the other conspirators found out that their plot had foundered, and Fawkes arrested, Catesby tried to rouse other Catholics to rise up with him. This didn't work out either, and he and the other plotters fled to Holbeche House. There, soldiers found them, a fight ensued and Catesby was killed. The others were hauled down to London to await their punishment. The men were all subjected to the traditional hanging, drawing and quartering. It certainly was severe, but the crime – treason – was considered really reprehensible. Fawkes, his body broken from torture, managed to jump off the scaffold, breaking his neck, and thus saved himself from the excruciating agonies that were to follow.

So, next time you hear someone labelling Guy Fawkes an anarchist – you know better. Catholics, who were already being persecuted, suffered more unpopularity as a result of the Gunpowder Plot, and were demonised throughout the rest of the period.

11. Women Didn't Wear Knickers

Although this fact may come as a surprise, most women in the Stuart period didn't wear knickers or panties (Samuel Pepys' wife, Elizabeth, wore 'drawers', but this was not common). Much like in the Tudor period before, Stuart women wore an article of clothing called a shift – which can also be called a chemise or smock. A shift would generally be a long-sleeved, long shirted T-shaped garment that would end under the knee or mid-calf. There were gussets, or square or rectangular-shaped pieces of fabric under the underarms to facilitate movement. The entire garment would have been made from linen or cotton and sewn with linen or silk thread. As with most clothing, the richer a person was the more luxurious the fabric. There is a particularly fine example of a smock dating from 1615–30 at the V&A Museum in London, which has beautiful embroidery of flowers, butterflies, and birds along the chest and some bobbin lace.

The undergarments were important because people didn't wash their clothes (nor their bodies) as regularly as we tend to do now, and the shift would be washed more regularly. Wealthier women would wear a new shift daily and theirs would usually have more embellishments than poorer women's shifts. So what did women do during their time of the month? They probably wore linen rags, which they would then wash, dry and reuse. On top of the shift, women would wear their stays – a shaping, supportive garment. Some clothing would have stays sewn into the bodice so these didn't require the same additional support.

12. The Stuart Family Had a Nasty Habit of Losing Their Heads

Gruesome and savage, decapitation rightly fills most people with horror and disgust. In the Early Modern period, however, beheading was considered the most respectful way of administering death to a person of high rank. Within the Stuart family in the seventeenth century, nearly every other generation following Mary, Queen of Scots had a significant member of the family beheaded.

Mary, Queen of Scots, the popular matriarch of the Stuart dynasty, had one of the most scandalous lives of the Tudor period. She is often referred to as a woman who followed her heart instead of her head, and this may be too unkind. Mary Stuart was born in 1542 in Linlithgow Palace, Scotland, to the French princess Mary of Guise and King James V of Scotland. James's mother was Margaret Tudor, a sister of Henry VIII of England. Six days after Mary's birth, her father died; this untimely event made her the Queen of Scots. She later moved to France and married Francis, Dauphin of France, and then became his Queen consort. Following Francis's untimely death at fifteen, Mary returned to her native Scotland. She chose to wed her cousin Lord Darnley, which was probably one of the worst decisions she made. However, with Darnley she gave birth to a son, James. Following Darnley's murder, she then married the Earl of Bothwell; following this, she was imprisoned in England for nineteen years. There, she was found guilty of conspiring to assassinate her cousin Queen Elizabeth and was beheaded at Fotheringhay Castle, Northamptonshire, in 1587.

Mary's grandson, Charles I, was beheaded outside

the Banqueting House of Whitehall Palace in January 1649. Charles's reign was significant because of the terrible and bloody civil wars that raged throughout his three kingdoms. Charles, whose reign had been a mixture of troubles mingled in with major personal blunders on his part, went to his death with great courage and dignity. Upon the scaffold, he told Bishop Juxon, 'I go from a corruptible to an incorruptible crown, where no disturbance can be, no disturbance in all the world.'

On Tower Hill today there are three plaques commemorating those who died on that hill throughout history. The most notable of the Early Modern period include those executed during the reign of the Tudors: Saint Thomas More, Thomas Cromwell, and Guilford Dudley. This same place of execution continued to be used during the reign of the Stuarts and figures such as the controversial William Laud, Archbishop of Canterbury, and, later, Colonel Algernon Sidney met their ends here. Charles I's grandson, James Scott, Duke of Monmouth, was also beheaded on Tower Hill in 1685 following his failed attempt to seize the throne from his uncle, James II.

Not all Stuarts who lost their heads lost them to the executioner's axe. A cannonball decapitated James FitzJames, 1st Duke of Berwick, an illegitimate son of James II and Arabella Churchill, during the siege of Philipsbourg in 1734.

13. Samuel Pepys Was a Lusty Fellow

Samuel Pepys (pronounced *Peeps*) is one of the most popular of historical figures from the Restoration, indeed of the seventeenth century. While he is now mostly known for his *Diary* (which he wrote in code), during his lifetime he was a naval clerk and later secretary of the Admiralty during the reigns of Charles II and James II. However, when William and Mary came to the throne, there was a major scandal about the costly neglect of some ships. This negligence and the subsequent controversy led to much finger-pointing and accusation. This necessitated the only work he published during his lifetime, *Memoires of the Royal Navy*, in 1689. This is extremely dry in comparison to his *Diary* but is nevertheless important because of the political scene in which its publishing proved necessary.

Pepys's *Diary*, on the other hand, has proved to be one of the most popular writings of the seventeenth century, and yet it was never intended to be read by anyone other than himself. Pepys wrote it in code in order to keep his thoughts private – and with good reason. Pepys was a man who went after pleasures of all kinds – he absolutely loved food, fashion, music and going to the theatre. The pleasures of the flesh were merely part of his ebullient character and his lust for life. Unlike some of his oversexed contemporaries, Pepys was not always successful when it came to attracting the opposite sex.

As documented in his *Diary*, there were many instances in which Pepys lusted after women (other than his wife, Elizabeth). There can be no doubt that he ogled, he fondled, he groped and more, but the label of 'pervert' some have applied to Pepys may stem not only from his womanising. On his birthday in 1669, he kissed the mouth of the long-dead corpse of Queen Catherine of Valois.

There is an instance where Pepys got frisky with a woman during a church service and she, being none too pleased about his wandering hands, threatened to prick him with one of her clothes pins. Pepys also had a bit of hopeless crush on Barbara, Lady Castlemaine, and an admiration for Nell Gwynn. Ship carpenter William Bagwell's wife aroused Pepys's lust. He led her to believe that if she granted him sexual favours then he would help her husband get a better ship.

Probably the most memorable naughty episodes in his diary involved his pursuit of Deb Willet, his wife's companion. A companion was a person who provided friendship and companionship for a lonely person. Unfortunately, Deb soon attracted Samuel's attention. Elizabeth, '*coming up suddenly, did find me embracing the girl with my hand under her petticoats; and indeed I was with my hand in her. I was at a wonderful loss upon it and the girl also …*' Caught in the act! Oh, Pepys!

14. Rich or Poor – Parasites Did Not Discriminate

One of the most unsavoury facts of the Stuart Era is that most people during this time had to deal with parasites such as fleas on a regular basis. Rich or poor, high-born or low, everyone had to deal with fleas, lice, and even intestinal worms! Even kings were not immune. Some people, including King Charles II, took preventative steps to reduce the chances of lice infestations by shaving the hair from their heads and covering up with wigs. Some wigs, however, contained nits and were teeming with parasitic life. The diarist Samuel Pepys was really put out with one wig-maker when he found that one of his costly new wigs was full of nits.

Fleas are generally believed to have been the conduit by which plague was transmitted, and several diseases are linked to them. While they were a major daily irritation, seventeenth-century persons could still find that there was something admirable in the flea's resilience. English polymath Robert Hooke described the flea thus: 'The strength and beauty of this small creature, had it no other relation at all to man, would deserve a description.' The flea, as a vessel containing blood, could be surprisingly erotic, as you can see in this excerpt from John Donne's metaphysical poem, *The Flea*. 'Mark but this flea, and mark in this, How little that which thou deniest me is; It suck'd me first, and now sucks thee, And in this flea our two bloods mingled be.'

Lice, both head lice and body lice, were another constant problem of daily life in the Stuart era. Lice, which are easily transmitted from person to person, were also harbingers of contagion and typhus was a common disease they spread. Fine-toothed combs were helpful in delousing hair. There have been archaeological excavations that have uncovered Early Modern combs that still have nits in between the teeth. Trouble didn't stop with fleas and lice, however, for intestinal worms were a common problem as well. These would make life very uncomfortable. The study of parasitical worms, helminthology, started to get going in the seventeenth century thanks to the use of microscopes, which revealed quite a lot of things that humans had never known about before.

Many people also slept on mattresses of hay, which were usually filled with other parasites (including bedbugs) that would feast upon them during the night while they slept. Also, if people had livestock animals such as pigs, they were usually able to wander around the house. Ticks were also around during the seventeenth century. Oh, and I nearly forgot about the leeches! These slug-like parasites were a Stuart-era physician's friend. Bloodletting was commonly used to treat fevers and these little babies were used to purify the blood. When a leech sucks enough blood, it separates from the host. Leeches are still used today after certain medical procedures.

As you can see, life in the Stuart era meant parasites were a human's constant companions. I don't know about you, but I'm a little itchy now.

15. The Royal Society Was Founded by Some of the Brightest of the Stuart Age

The Stuart era was a remarkable period for scientific endeavour in which human curiosity mixed with reason and philosophy with experimentation. The Royal Society was founded during the reign of King Charles II and is undoubtedly one of the greatest contributions to our world. Edmund Halley, Robert Hooke, William Petty, Robert Boyle, Isaac Newton, Elias Ashmole, Christopher Wren, were all a dream-team of physicists, natural philosophers, mathematicians and brilliant minds. Some people are apt to disparage the inclusion of royals in this list, but it would be silly to omit them because Charles, James, and especially Rupert had a great interest in science; the latter proved to be one of the most active members of the Society. Although the full origins and members of the Royal Society are still a source of controversy in the academic community, it was founded on 28 November 1660, the first meeting being at Gresham College.

The Royal Society debated a wide variety of scientific topics including ventilation, bees, planetary movements and the properties of light and physics. Although a small number of people tend to disparage the achievements of the gentlemen-scientists of the Stuart age, one must remember that gentlemen in this period were encouraged to take an interest in a variety of things, and this is why so many men from this and the subsequent century pulled off that rare move of being very good at several pursuits. They may have been the greatest minds of the Stuart age, but that didn't stop them from bickering among themselves.

Newton had quite a few quarrels with his colleagues, especially Robert Hooke. Wren, on the other hand, was so good-natured that he got on well with most of his colleagues.

Some of the Society's experiments included activities such as incubating chickens' eggs and observing comets (such as the Great Comet of 1664), and several members including Christopher Wren and Robert Boyle performed intravenous experiments on live dogs. In 1661, Robert Boyle published *The Sceptical Chymist*, but he's best known for Boyle's Law from 1662, which states that the pressure of a gas is inversely proportional to the volume when at a fixed temperature, or PV = k.

It is no wonder that NASA and ESA have named several missions, planets, asteroids, etc. after some of great seventeenth-century scientists. These include the Galilean moons (named after Galileo Galilei), the Kepler Mission (after Johannes Kepler), XMM-Newton (after Isaac Newton) and the Cassini-Huygens spacecraft (after Giovanni Domenico Cassini and Christiaan Huygens). Although some of these figures were not in the Royal Society, their ideas and research impacted the work of those who were.

16. Some People Thought Orange Juice Was Dangerous

International trade made possible by companies such as the Dutch East India Company brought strange and wonderful foods as a result of their exploration (and some exploitation) of far-flung lands. Some of these include everyday items that many now take for granted: pineapples, drinking chocolate, tea, and coffee. I've looked in my kitchen cupboard and found all sorts of dried herbs and spices. The latter were quite costly back in the day, especially nutmeg – the trade in which was dominated by the Dutch.

While these are normal household groceries now, seventeenth-century people were sometimes wary of trying these new foods and beverages. The diarist and naval administrator Samuel Pepys documented his concerns before drinking his first-ever orange juice. On 9 of March 1668/9, Pepys had a go. 'And here, which I never did before, I drank a glass, of a pint, I believe, at one draught, of the juice of oranges, of whose peel they make comfits; and here they drink the juice as wine, with sugar, and it is very fine drink; but, it being new, I was doubtful whether it might not do me hurt.' Needless to say, the pint-glassful of orange juice didn't kill him. By 1699, however, orange juice was considered safe; Pepys's friend John Evelyn recommended it as an ingredient in a few of the recipes in his *Acetaria*.

Bananas, considered a staple breakfast food now, were never seen in England before 1633, when it was sold in London. As for drinking chocolate, we have the Irishman Hans Sloane to thank for that, for he first tried the beverage in Jamaica and brought it to

England. Solid chocolate candy wasn't around until the mid-nineteenth century. Ice cream was also introduced to Britain in the Stuart period, and this incredible novelty was often served to Charles I. Gin was also introduced.

The Stuarts ate all manner of things that many today would find unappetising. Pigeon pie would have been made with pigeon meat, and cock ale was made by stewing a chicken in fermenting beer to create a beverage that was believed to be most nourishing. Salads tentatively began to appear, especially with enthusiastic proponents such as John Evelyn. Potages were a typical dish on the Stuart table. A potage could be made in a variety of ways, but it usually contained oatmeal, broth, herbs, and could be made with any meat that was available – chicken, mutton, or pigeon. Water during the Stuart period was of dubious cleanliness and so most people drank small beer – even children (it was not strongly alcoholic). In order to make beer, water was boiled which killed bacteria. White bread historically was something only wealthier people could afford to buy. For example, in March of 1665, a 'Wheaten' loaf of bread was a penny, but a 'White Loaf', weighing the same amount as the brown loaf, was as much as three and a half pennies!

17. William Harvey Discovered Blood Circulation

Greek physician Galen (*c.* 129–*c.* 216/17 CE) was a major early physician whose works were integral to medicine from his time up to the Early Modern period. Galen's beliefs about the human body and medicine were, in turn, heavily influenced by Hippocrates – an earlier Greek physician and philosopher from whom we get the Hippocratic oath, among other things. Galen incorrectly believed that the veins came from the liver.

That was all well and good until Kentish physician William Harvey made the monumental discovery that blood circulates throughout the body. Born in the Elizabethan age in 1578, he was both financially privileged and naturally intelligent enough to warrant going to university. (Harvey, a Royalist, eventually became a royal physician to both James I and Charles I, and during the English Civil War, he observed the Battle of Edgehill in 1642.) He even studied abroad at the much-respected University of Padua, where he studied under Hieronymus Fabricius, who in turn had studied under Andreas Vesalius.

The latter was a highly influential anatomist in the sixteenth century, and he is notable because he found fault with certain aspects of Galen's work; this was made evident in his 1543 work, entitled *On the Fabric of the Human Body*. Galenic medicine, although an ancient system, had gone largely unchallenged for centuries. William Harvey was going to turn the medical world upside down. In contrast to Galen's beliefs, Harvey theorised that it was the heart and not the liver that was the source from which the veins emanated.

In 1628, Harvey published his findings in *Exercitatio Anatomica de Motu Cordis et Sanguinis in Animalibus*. His work was met with the standard mixture of criticism and agreement. Some critics simply wouldn't accept a deviation from Galenic principles. Being a proponent of such a radical new theory had its drawbacks. According to biographer John Aubrey in his *The Natural History of Wiltshire*, 'In those times to have had an inventive and enquiring wit was accounted affectation which censure the famous Dr William Harvey could not escape for his admirable discovery of the circulation of the blood.'

Almost a decade later, in 1636, he went over to the University of Altdorf on the Continent, where he gave a lecture on anatomy. He brought in a live dog and cut him open to show the heart. This was a time before any notion of animal rights was around, and so he tested his theory on living animals. Although we see this as cruel now, how else could he have observed and demonstrated his theory? Even if the ends did not justify the means, Harvey's discovery had a huge impact on medicine, and no doubt this has saved lives in the long run. Towards the end of his life, the Parliamentarians hounded Harvey. When soldiers ransacked his house, many of his research papers were lost or destroyed. He died following a stroke in 1657.

18. The Restoration Rakes Were Oversexed, Overdressed and Over-the-Top

Those of a more gentle persuasion, look away now! The Restoration Age is known as a bawdy era, and with good reason. Oversexed, overdressed and over-the-top, the libertines of the Restoration era remain some of the most popular bad boys in history. With their ostentatious suits (the original *'Three Piece Suit'*), fine lace cravats at their chin and curled periwigs, these handsome aristocrats were lascivious heartbreakers. They whiled away their hours in gambling at card tables and placing bets at the horseraces, they indulged every conceivable sexual whim at the whorehouses and debauched the young ladies of the court, and when they drank, they downed copious quantities of whatever alcoholic beverage was around.

Who were these men who led such depraved lifestyles? King Charles II, himself a notoriously lovable lecher, was often surrounded by equally profligate friends who were called the Merry Gang. Some of these men were also in Charles's Cabal ministry. George Villiers, 2nd Duke of Buckingham, was the son of the 1st Duke of Buckingham, and this roué had an affair with a married woman, killed her husband in a duel and lived in a *ménage à trois*. Charles Sackville, 6th Earl of Dorset, was another lothario and he took Nell Gwynn as his mistress before she became the king's.

James, Duke of York, was Charles's younger brother, and he also had quite a sexual appetite. Unlike most of the other restoration rakes, however, James had the (mis)fortune of having a conscience. He was hopelessly unfaithful to both of his wives, Anne Hyde and Mary of Modena. James's two most well-known mistresses were Arabella Churchill and Catherine Sedley, neither of whom were considered beauties. The latter of the two was the daughter of one of the most infamous of the rakes ...

Sir Charles Sedley is most infamously known for his sexually explicit stunt on a balcony in Covent Garden. Samuel Pepys recorded in his *Diary* how Sedley had stood stark naked on a balcony and pretended to sodomise another man, and then he proceeded to make lewd comments at the large crowd of spectators below and then, in front of everyone, washed his penis in a glass of red wine. After that, he drank the contents of the glass! Sedley also sent a few thugs armed with sticks to beat up the actor Ned Kynaston. In spite of these antics, bizarrely, Sedley managed to attract the popular Restoration actress Margaret Hughes, who was his mistress for a few years (and then she upgraded to Stuart hunk Prince Rupert of the Rhine).

They made merry, but most contracted some type of venereal disease such as the 'French Pox' (syphilis). Although there were condoms in use, they were nowhere near as good as modern condoms in preventing pregnancy or sexual diseases. They also needed soaking in milk or water to render them pliable for use. These Restoration rakes fathered many bastards. As for Wilmot, well, he gets his own entry.

19. The Bank of England Was Founded in 1694 … and Created the National Debt

King William III's most pressing mission in his life was to thwart French King Louis XIV from further expansion. For most of his life, William had the constant concern that the French would conquer his country, the Dutch Republic. In 1672, known as the *Rampjaar* or 'Disaster Year', the French attacked and many lives were lost. The only way to stop Louis XIV was to engage in constant warfare against the French aggressor until the latter was soundly defeated. William's wars understandably proved extremely costly, and by the early 1690s the royal coffers were already running dry. William needed money, and he needed it as soon as possible.

Various financial schemes began to get floated about in an effort to solve this problem, and King William approved of one in particular. Scottish entrepreneur William Paterson concocted a system in which a large loan would be made to the government at a rate of 8 per cent interest. Charles Montagu, 1st Earl of Halifax, William and Mary's Chancellor of the Exchequer, was a major proponent of this scheme. All that was left was official royal approval, and on 24 July 1694, William and Mary founded the Bank of England.

The creation of the Bank of England was not only a matter of economics but of politics. After the Glorious Revolution of 1688, two distinct political groups came to the forefront, the Tories and the Whigs, and if there is anything about the political spectrum of the Late Stuart courts you need to know, it's that these two groups did not get on well together. An overwhelming majority of those involved in the creation of the Bank of England were Whigs. Montagu, importantly, was a Whig. Robert Harley, who later became the Chancellor of the Exchequer under Queen Anne, became a notable critic of the Bank of England and created the rival Tory Land Bank (I did mention that they didn't get along). Nineteenth-century historian G. M. Trevelyan stated that the Bank of England was established 'against the opposition of the Tories, who were jealous of the monied interest'. The first Governor of the Bank of England (from 1694–7) was John Houblon, and he was also a director in the New East India Company. This company was very much a Whig-heavy company – once again adding to the political nature of the entire financial setup.

£1.2 million was raised as the loan. This debt was never repaid and became the roots of what we call the National Debt. By 1700, only six years after the Bank of England had been founded, the debt had risen to £12 million. This is nothing in comparison to what it is today; in the 2010s, the National Debt exceeded £1 trillion – an astronomical sum its creators could never possibly have imagined. As for William defeating the French, well, that victory would be posthumous and Queen Anne would get the credit when John Churchill and Prince Eugene of Savoy teamed up and thrashed Louis' army at the Battle of Blenheim in 1704.

20. Charles I Was the Spare Who Became the Heir

While possibly not the nicest phrase to use, this situation wasn't an extraordinary occurrence in history. After all, Henry VIII was another example of a second son that became an heir, following his elder brother Prince Arthur's death in 1502. King Charles I was very different from Henry VIII and has gone down in British history as one of the most controversial and hated monarchs and yet, he was never supposed to have been king in the first place. Charles was the younger brother of Henry, Prince of Wales, and upon the latter's death in 1612, the former was the 'spare who became the heir'.

Henry Frederick Stuart, born in Stirling Castle, Scotland, in 1594, was by all accounts the epitome of what an Early Modern prince should be: learned, athletic, intelligent, handsome, confident, fashionable – you name it, he had it. As the eldest son of King James I and Anne of Denmark, Henry was the beloved golden boy in the family and his staunchly Protestant, sober court put his father's to shame. His morals were much admired; swearing was a punishable offence and drunkenness frowned upon.

In late 1612, Henry suddenly came down with a terrible illness – which modern historians now believe to have been typhoid fever – and the handsome, robust eighteen-year-old died. Indeed, the tragic prince's early and sudden demise sent shockwaves across the nation – for in him, all hopes of future stability had depended. Henry Stuart is one of those figures in history that historians think of with that hopeless question, 'What if?' Would the English Civil Wars have happened had he lived to be king? Charles, once the 'spare', was then violently thrust into the role of heir – a position for which he was neither fully prepared nor as good at as his deceased brother.

Charles, now the heir, was considered the runt of the family for he had been a sickly child, suffering from both rickets and a pronounced stutter. But Charles was not without virtues of his own. Quite like Henry had been, Charles was very cultivated and had a great passion for art. He became a great collector of art and a major patron to artists, most famously Flemish Baroque painters Anthony van Dyck and Peter Paul Rubens. The former painted many portraits of King Charles, including the ubiquitous equestrian portraits. Rubens is best known for the sumptuous and symbolically rich paintings that adorn the ceiling in the Banqueting House, Whitehall.

Charles was also a devoted and loving family man; there can be no question of his attachment to his wife, Henrietta Maria, or their six children together. He was the opposite of his son Charles II in that Charles had an awful combination of stubbornness, a firmly entrenched belief in the Divine Right of Kings and the unfortunate ability to go along with whatever the last person advised him to do. Some historians state that Charles I's finest moment was the time of his execution. He met his death bravely.

21. The Reign of William and Mary Was the Only Diarchy in British History

Usually a monarch rules on his or her own – as was the case with Henry V and later Elizabeth I – and that makes a monarchy. Thus, when a king marries, his wife becomes the Queen *consort* – meaning not a queen in her own right. Anne Boleyn, for example, was Henry VIII's consort. Queen regnant, which is what their daughter Elizabeth became, means a queen rules in her own right. Queen Victoria was the same, and although she was married to Albert, he never became king and remained prince consort. Queen Elizabeth II is a queen regnant, and her husband, Prince Philip, Duke of Edinburgh, remained a prince consort.

In the unique circumstance of William and Mary, the latter was the heir and was well within her right to rule as Queen Mary II and have her husband, William, as her prince consort. But Mary was very much a woman of her time – and very well respected for it – and she refused to become queen if William wasn't king. She thought it highly unnatural that a woman should rule over her husband. William was half a Stuart too, as his mother was Charles I's eldest daughter, who was also named Mary; his claim to the throne was legitimate, although not as strong as his wife's. In April 1689, they became joint rulers and the diarchy of William and Mary began. Their reign remains unique in British history – there has been no other before or since. This diarchy lasted only five years as Mary died in 1694, leaving William to rule alone.

22. Highwaymen and Footpads Made Journeys Perilous

The Stuart period was a time in which occasional violence was a fact of life. In the *Bills of Mortality*, it was common to find 'found dead in the street' or 'murdered', so that gives us a pretty good idea of what it was like. Although most people had jobs – from mop seller to night-soil man to scullery maid and oyster seller – there was an underworld, one of crime and viciousness. In striking contrast to the romanticised notion many people now have of highwaymen and footpads, these criminals were very dangerous. A highwayman (usually on horseback) would stop travellers on the road and rob them at gunpoint. While not as common, there were also female highwaymen, including Moll 'Cutpurse' Frith. There were several Acts passed by parliament throughout the Stuart era in an attempt to clamp down on these criminals. There is one Act from 1652 against highwaymen and another in 1692 under William and Mary, which shows that the problem was bad throughout most of the century.

A footpad was the seventeenth-century equivalent of a mugger. Some places became notorious for footpads and cutpurses, one of these being Blackheath, an area situated close to the Royal Observatory in Greenwich. Footpads were a problem all over the place but particularly in areas where they knew they could get a wealthy victim. Hyde Park was known for attracting these nasty types. Accordingly, the Route du Roi, or Rotten Row, which was a road that led from Kensington Palace to Whitehall, was ordered by William III to be lined with lamps. The road was completed in 1690 and is generally regarded as the first lighted road in England.

23. Shakespeare Left Us the Greatest Works in the English Language ... and an Enduring Controversy

Arguably the greatest writer in all history, let alone British history, William Shakespeare has become a sort of demigod to admirers of his sonnets and plays. Born in 1564 in Stratford-upon-Avon, this son of a glover eventually travelled to London and became an actor and playwright. Shakespeare had an amazing range – able to write high-spirited plays such as *A Midsummer Night's Dream* as well as extremely violent dark tragedy, such as *Titus Andronicus*. He wrote the long poems *Venus and Adonis* and *The Rape of Lucrece*, both dedicated to his patron the Earl of Southampton. Several of Shakespeare's plays were performed before royalty, Queen Elizabeth (who died in 1603) and her successor, King James I. Shakespeare, having left us with the brilliance that is *Hamlet*, *Macbeth*, *Much Ado About Nothing*, *The Tempest*, *Romeo and Juliet*, *Othello* and many more, died in 1616.

Since then, there have been those who have questioned whether Shakespeare was actually the author of the works that are so beloved to so many people. Indeed, this topic can get some people really riled up. The Shakespeare Authorship Question leads to divided beliefs, and the most popular fall into the following categories: the Oxfordians, the Baconians, and the Stratfordians. Those who adhere to the Oxfordian theory claim the true author to be Edward de Vere, 17th Earl of Oxford, who was unable to publicly claim authorship because of being a nobleman. Others, the Baconians, believe Shakespeare was really Francis Bacon, Viscount St. Albans, who was an extremely intelligent philosopher and scientist who developed the Baconian method. The Stratfordians maintain that William Shakespeare was the sole author of the works attributed to him. Others believe the works were the result of collaborative efforts by several writers, including Marlowe. Even more think the whole notion of any controversy is downright absurd. Others think it intellectually snobbish to presume that someone who didn't go to university would be incapable of writing Shakespeare's works.

Whatever the reader's personal beliefs are about this matter, the fact remains that the works attributed to William Shakespeare are some of the greatest works in the English language. After Shakespeare's death, a few of his plays were published, but these publications were not known for their good quality. Thirty-six of his plays were published in 1623 in what is known as the First Folio. The title page of this publication contains one of the most popular images of Shakespeare. First Folio editions are extremely precious books, and copies are found at some of the most prestigious institutions in the world, including the Bodleian Library at the University of Oxford, the British Library and the Folger Shakespeare Library in Washington, D.C. Three subsequent Folios of Shakespeare's works were published in the Stuart period, in 1632, 1663 and 1685.

Throughout London, visitors can see monuments dedicated to him, such as the fountain in the middle of Leicester Square, and the beautiful memorial to him at Southwark Cathedral. As for any controversy, well, to quote Shakespeare himself, 'it's all Greek to me'.

24. Witchcraft Was a Very Serious Matter

Witchcraft, particularly in the early seventeenth century, was a very real concern for many people. This was a time in which people were much more religious and superstitious than most are in the twenty-first century. Outbreaks of plague and other diseases, combined with poor harvests and the misery of hunger, led to social problems including accusations of witchcraft. Personal or economic tragedies and misfortunes were usually interpreted as stemming from a supernatural cause. Generally speaking, angry, fearful people needed a scapegoat, so who better than the weird old and ugly woman who lived alone in the village? The odd one out in a parish was more than likely to be accused and condemned.

There were several notable witch trials, including those of the Pendle Witches and the Samlesbury witches, both in 1612. Even King James I wrote *Daemonologie* in 1597. Yes, this was the same King James who commissioned the King James Bible, in which you'll find Exodus 22:18 (KJV): 18 – 'Thou shalt not suffer a witch to live'. It was this line that had a direct impact on many trials. Although James was the opposite of a warmonger-king and was tolerant for his time, he was nevertheless a major witch-hunter. There is no exact number of those who were accused and put to death for witchcraft, but estimates generally run into the tens of thousands, if not higher.

The 'Witchfinder-General' was one Matthew Hopkins, who was the author of the 1647 pamphlet *The Discovery of Witches*. Contrary to popular belief, Hopkins was not authorised by the government to do what he did – he gave himself that title. Hopkins went around East Anglia, trying people for witchcraft using some really horrible methods, including the swimming test. No one could really stop him because he was operating during the chaos of the English Civil Wars. Generally, if you were unfortunate enough to be accused of being a witch, you would die proving your innocence. A common myth is that those found guilty of witchcraft in the seventeenth century were burned. Unlike previous centuries, in which burning was used to kill so-called 'witches', in the seventeenth century, the method employed was most often hanging.

In the Restoration, the puritan influence, which had been so dominant in earlier decades, decreased. While the strong fears of witchcraft had reduced considerably, however, they had not altogether vanished. The most infamous late flare-up was the Salem Witch Trials, which took place across the Atlantic in the Massachusetts Bay Colony in 1692.

As the Stuart era came to an end, belief in witchcraft began to go into decline. The Enlightenment values of reason and evidence began to take hold and shake off the cobwebs of superstition and irrationality. Charles II and William III were very sceptical in comparison with their ancestor James I, and perhaps this royal scepticism had a trickle-down effect on the population as a whole.

25. New York Used to Be New Amsterdam

Ah, the Big Apple. New York City is one of the greatest cities in the world, and yet it wasn't always known as New 'York'. Before the ubiquitous yellow taxis, Statue of Liberty, and Times Square, Manhattan was once a seventeenth-century Dutch colony called New Amsterdam. Even before that, however, it was Native American land. The original inhabitants of this area were the Lenni-Lenape, before the Dutch settled. The Dutch West India Company (as opposed to its much more famous Dutch East India Company) founded New Amsterdam on this island in 1625. The Dutch had amazingly lucrative trading routes across the world. From the crucial location of New Amsterdam, the Dutch were able to get another valuable commodity: fur.

In the 1660s, Anglo-Dutch relations weren't terrible, but they weren't particularly good either. After all, the First Anglo-Dutch war had ended during Cromwell's time. Charles II decided he wanted some of that Dutch trade for England. The governor of New Amsterdam was one Peter Stuyvesant, who was by some accounts an irritable man who was strongly disliked as a result. When the English invaded (Charles had sent four men-of-war over to the New World, commanded by Richard Nicholls), Stuyvesant had little choice but to surrender to the English, which took place on 8 September 1664. New Amsterdam was renamed New York after James, Duke of York (who later became King James II). Even after the Second Anglo-Dutch War, which naturally followed the renewed hostilities between both nations, the English were able to keep New York.

26. Plague Doctors Weren't Always Doctors

Plague had been a huge problem in Europe since the fourteenth century, when the Black Death swept through the lands, decimating populations in its wake. Black rats were for many years blamed for spreading the disease. Recent research suggests that gerbils from Asia, and not black rats, were responsible for carrying the disease. The Great Plague of 1665 greatly impacted the country. The eerie herb-stuffed beak mask, the cloak and the gloves of the plague doctor made for a striking, if not frightening, image. Many people might assume that the term 'plague doctors' meant that these individuals were trained physicians, but this was simply not the case.

Poorly paid and exposed to the deadly contagion, these 'doctors' were usually anyone that could be found to do the job as many of the real physicians fled London once the plague outbreak grew worse. Indeed, it was hard to find anyone other than those from the criminal underworld who had nothing to lose and maybe a little to gain. Plague nurses were no better. Most of these were equally untrustworthy and would eventually steal what they could find of value from their dying patients. Their duties were to look after those suffering from the plague, by feeding them, etc. Plague searchers were people entrusted to remove dead bodies from where they were found and take them to plague pits, where the plague victims were buried. Almost a quarter of London's population perished because of the plague.

27. The 'Bloodless' Glorious Revolution Definitely Wasn't Bloodless

When people talk about the Glorious Revolution of 1688, the word 'bloodless' gets thrown around a lot. While it is indeed true that there was little bloodshed in England, there were some very bloody battles in both Scotland and Ireland that came as a direct result of the revolution. While we cannot go into great detail about these battles, these were important because they secured William and Mary on the throne. The revision of names for historical events has permeated (or plagued!) the academic community since around the 1970s (the *English Civil War* is now referred to as *The Wars of the Three Kingdoms*, the *Wars of the Roses* is now *The Cousins' War*, etc.) and there are some who argue that the 'Glorious Revolution' should be called something else, but for the sake of consistency, we'll keep the traditional name.

In Ireland, there were several major battles associated with the Glorious Revolution, the most famous being the Battle of the Boyne, which was fought in 1690 near Drogheda, Ireland. The Williamite forces crossed the River Boyne and fought with the Jacobites. Over a thousand died. This battle is often claimed to have been the one that won the war for the Williamites, and that's both true and false. The battle that definitely ensured things were in William's favour was the Battle of Aughrim in 1691, which usually gets ignored but is no less important. When Richard Talbot, 1st Earl of Tyrconnell, learned the news of this defeat, he suffered a stroke and died a few days later.

In Scotland, there was the Battle of Killiecrankie of

1689, which gave the Jacobites a pyrrhic victory. The leader of this Jacobite rebellion was John Claverhouse, Viscount Dundee, known affectionately as 'Bonnie Dundee', but his death at Killiecrankie severely impacted morale and the Williamite forces ultimately gained control. Next came the Glencoe Massacre of 1692, which remains a controversial and painful event for the Scots. However, some remained loyal to James. Due to several unfortunate circumstances, the MacDonalds of Glencoe were late in giving their oath, and the Master of Stair showed no mercy. As punishment, the same soldiers who had been enjoying MacDonald hospitality for several days followed the orders they were given and slaughtered many of their hosts – including the clan chief. Survivors, mainly women, children and the elderly, soon died of exposure in the freezing wilderness during that harsh winter of 1692. The Massacre of Glencoe severely tarnished William's reputation in history. Although whether he actually meant for the massacre to happen can never be known, he did not punish but instead gave good positions to those involved. It must be mentioned, however, that a similarly ruthless incident occurred in the Dutch Republic in 1672, when the De Witt brothers were savagely murdered and mutilated by a pro-Orangist mob. As you can see, the Glorious Revolution was decidedly bloody, not bloodless.

28. Diarist John Evelyn Was a Salad Fiend

John Evelyn (1620–1706), the second-most famous diarist of the seventeenth century after Samuel Pepys, was a man of many talents. Although Evelyn and Pepys were good friends and moved in the same circles, they were different. Evelyn was a more cerebral man, who enjoyed practical pursuits, while Pepys was drawn to the sensuous side of life. Evelyn's *Diary* remains one of the most informative accounts of major historical events in the Stuart Age, and therefore is of great importance to researchers. The manuscripts are now in the possession of the British Library in London. Evelyn was not just an enthusiastic diarist but a keen gardener as well, and his house at Sayes Court, near Deptford, was known for its beautiful gardens. These gardens, and especially Evelyn's precious bushes, were quite badly damaged during Peter the Great's stay (worth reading about in itself).

He was an early kind of environmentalist, although to refer to him as such may be a little over-simplistic. Evelyn's *Fumifugium; Or, the Inconvenience of the Aer and Smoake of London* pamphlet, published in 1661, is important because it shows his concern about the levels of pollution in London's air. In this, he stated that Londoners 'breathe nothing but an impure and thick Mist accompanied with a fuliginous and filthy vapour'. In another pamphlet of his, entitled *Sylva, Or A Discourse of Forest Trees and the Propagation of Timber In His Majesty's Dominions*, he stated that 'such woods as do yet remain entire, might be carefully preserved, and such as are destroy'd, sedulously repaired'. Evelyn also wrote *Terra: A Philosophical*

Essay of Earth. Although he was a little long-winded in some respects in his pamphlets, he nevertheless gave some good advice.

One of the lesser-known things about Evelyn is that he was very keen on salads, or *sallats*, as he spelled them. The typical diet of a man in his station would consist of a lot of meat, so it is interesting to see there were those who didn't like the meat-heavy diet of the time. Evelyn loved salads so much that he wrote a book entirely devoted to the art of salad making – *Acetaria: A Discourse of Sallats*. This fascinating book lists the various recipes one could use to make a salad, but also how to cultivate the many herbs and vegetables used in them. There are recipes for artichokes, beetroot (beets), cabbage, endives, lettuce, fennel, carrots, and cucumbers. For the latter, Evelyn recommends slicing them thinly and adding oil and lemon juice or vinegar. Garlic-lovers may be disappointed; Evelyn was not partial to it, going so far as to say that despite its reputation for being healthful, it has an 'intolerable rankness'.

Being an early salad-lover must have been good for his health; Evelyn lived to a ripe old age (nearly eighty-six!) and seems to have been largely illness-free. Although he claimed to have been a 'very moderate eater of them', I think we can safely say Evelyn was a salad fiend.

29. Rupert of the Rhine Was a Stuart-Era Renaissance Man

Prince Rupert of the Rhine was one of the many children of Elizabeth Stuart and Frederick V of the Palatinate. Born in Prague in December of 1619 during his parents' brief stint as the King and Queen of Bohemia, Rupert's life was adventure-filled from the very beginning. His parents had made a gamble, and in return had lost everything and were forced into exile. Rupert would eventually become a major military leader, a prisoner of war, a buccaneer, an inventor, an artist and a scientist.

Rupert was one of the greatest Cavalier/Royalist military leaders during the English Civil War. As Captain-General of the Royalist army, he cut a rather impressive figure both on and off the battlefield. Not only was he a skilled military leader, but also a scientist and an artist. Another charming aspect of his personality included his inclusion of his dog wherever he went. Boye was a white poodle that Rupert trained to urinate on command every time he heard the word 'Pym' (Pym was a major Parliamentarian figure).

When he failed to defend Bristol from the Parliamentarians, Rupert faced his uncle's extreme displeasure and was exiled. Rupert's younger brother Maurice is believed to have died in a shipwreck during a hurricane in the West Indies in 1652. This was a huge blow to the normally assertive man, and for years he continued to hope in vain that his brother was alive. Rupert's travels took him to the Caribbean, where he nearly died from the bloody flux.

Off the battlefield, Rupert was accomplished in a wide variety of things. A mezzotint of his, *The Great*

Executioner, from around 1658, is generally recognised to be a skilled example of this kind of art. (He also had a considerably large and artistic signature.) Rupert was a savant, and his innate curiosity led to his becoming one of the founders and most active members of The Royal Society. He had a natural excitement when it came to scientific experimentation, a fact which led to several discoveries and inventions, including his improvement of gunpowder, mine detonations and naval experiments. Towards the end of his rather long life, Rupert lived in Windsor Castle, where he worked on a variety of scientific experiments in a laboratory.

He was by his mother's side when she died in London in 1662. With his dimpled chin and striking good looks, Rupert didn't have trouble attracting the ladies. Although rumoured to have been married to the court beauty Frances Bard, who bore him a son, he appears to have remained a bachelor. Towards his later years, Rupert did have a relationship with the actress Margaret 'Peg' Hughes. He lavished jewels and gifts upon her. After a life of adventure, Prince Rupert died aged sixty-three in 1682 and was buried in Westminster Abbey. In his will, Rupert left his money and possessions to his 'naturelle' son Dudley Bard (with Frances), Margaret and their daughter, Ruperta. Rupert of the Rhine lived his life to the full, and even after 300 years, he still manages to send hearts a-flutter.

30. The French Set the Fashion for Nearly Everything

No surprises there, as the French have always been known for their style. Louis XIV of France and one of his mistresses made several big contributions to high-end Stuart fashion. First of all, King Louis loved Baroque ballet and in his youth he enjoyed dancing, but as he aged, he lost some of his youthful good looks. As his hair began to recede, he began to wear a wig. This periwig became the must-have accessory for the fashion-conscious, upper-class male. As the seventeenth-century came to a close, the periwigs had become more voluminous and ostentatious. But Louis' mark on the fashion world didn't end there. He was a little on the short side, so he began to wear high heeled shoes (modern fashionistas who praise Louboutin's red heels will do well to know that red heels were fashionable in Louis XIV's court first). Unfortunately, his courtiers copied him, making there little point in his having adopted the shoes in the first place. Even Louis' considerably taller cousin, Charles II, wore heels because they were so fashionable.

During the Restoration, French style was very popular in the Merry Monarch's court. Not everyone was impressed by the English court's adoption of French clothing, and courtier and writer John Evelyn was one of them. In order to hit back he wrote *Tyrannus, or The Mode in a discourse of sumptuary laws* in 1661. In this, Evelyn wrote that if a country allows the clothing and language of another, this is simply the beginning of a conquest. France and England had been historical enemies for hundreds of years, and so the average person was not comfortable with French fashions being so well-received among their leaders. As much as he liked France, Evelyn thought England should create its own fashions.

Next came the face patch. In a time of badly disfiguring diseases such as smallpox and syphilis, these little beauties were very much appreciated. Smallpox would leave pockmarks or pits on the skin, and face patches were used to cover these blemishes. Patches were made out of black fabric, from either taffeta, velvet, silk or paper, and applied to the face with gum. Patch boxes were a popular addition to a lady's dressing table. Mary II had a face-patch box, which was beautifully decorated in red and gold, surrounded by images of flowers and plants, and the lid featured her monogram and a crown. Even women who were blessed with rare undamaged skin wore them because they were so fashionable.

In the late Stuart era, a towering headdress became really trendy. The *Coiffure a la Fontanges* was named after the Duchesse de Fontanges, a young woman who was briefly a mistress of Louis XIV's. Hair was curled at the top of the head, the rest hidden away under a cap, a vertical structure of lace (usually white) would rise above the head, and two long pieces of lace would dangle past the neck. During the reigns of William and Mary and then Queen Anne, this headwear was congruent with the straighter, vertical fashions and was ubiquitous among noblewomen.

31. A Physician's 'Cures' Were Often Worse than the Disease

In the early Stuart era, medicine was very much a matter of the four humours – fire, air, water, and earth. That is to say, physicians believed all diseases came from an imbalance of the four elements, those being yellow bile, blood, phlegm and black bile. Humourism was popularised by the work of the ancient Greek physician and philosopher Galen. If a physician thought a person needed to vomit, they would sometimes give them a glass of urine mixed with salt. The thought alone is enough to make one queasy.

Fevers were a common problem, and somehow or other physicians got it into their heads that dead pigeons applied to a ill person's feet would draw the fever or 'vapours' down from their head and out through their feet. Pepys mentions a time when he was summoned to an ill man's bed and witnessed this, 'So I to him, and his breath rattled in the throat; and they did lay pigeons to his feet, and all despair of him.'

You'd be mistaken if you thought that the rich and powerful were exempt. If anything, they had it worse – they had the money to hire physicians. Medicine has come a long way since the Early Modern era. When Charles II suffered a stroke, described as a 'fit of apoplexy', in the winter of 1685, he was subjected to a horrendous set of cures from his physicians. His physicians bled him first (sixteen ounces first, then another eight!), shaved his head, blistered his flesh with hot irons and administered enemas. Nearly sixty different medicines were given to the ailing king. Ultimately, Charles II's last few days of life proved utterly torturous, and he died on 6 February 1685.

A similar sort of thing happened with Charles's cousin, Louis XIV. Stuart-era surgical operations were performed by barber-surgeons (at the time surgery was spelled *chirurgery*, surgeons were *chirurgeons*). Louis had a bad tooth removed. Now, those of us who've had teeth removed know that post-operative care is very important in order to reduce the risk of the infection or dry socket. Unfortunately, the socket that was left in Louis's mouth became infected and it was so painful that the dentists/physicians decided that they had to pull his top teeth out. All this was done without anaesthesia, so you can imagine the pain! This wasn't the only excruciating medical procedure Louis had to endure.

In 1686, the Sun King developed an anal fistula, which is an uncomfortable and oftentimes very painful medical condition in which a hole forms another passage in the skin around the anus. Waste can enter this wound and become infected, which is why (along with the sheer pain) that Louis's physicians decided something had to be done. A barber-surgeon named Felix was summoned but he tested the procedure out on French peasants first! Louis went through the ordeal, again without any anaesthetic, and survived.

32. St Paul's Cathedral Dominated London's Skyline for over 200 Years

The English Baroque masterpiece that is St Paul's Cathedral in London is one of the most iconic buildings in the world. It's been the venue for royal weddings (Prince Charles and Lady Diana Spencer), state funerals (Winston Churchill) and the resting place for some of the nation's great military heroes (such as Admiral Nelson). Before the current building's creation in the late seventeenth and early eighteenth centuries, however, the medieval St Paul's Cathedral was just as awe-inspiring. It was inside this St Paul's that the wedding of Arthur, Prince of Wales and Catherine of Aragon took place. St Paul's was also where John Donne gave his sermons during his time as the Dean of St Paul's.

With the 1640s came the civil war, and Parliamentarian troops used the cathedral as a place to stable their horses (the Roundheads did that quite often). It was so badly damaged and poorly maintained that at the Restoration there were plans to spruce it up and get it back to its former splendour. Christopher Wren proposed a design for a dome to rest atop the cathedral, topped by a strange amalgamation between a pinecone and a pineapple. All such plans came to a fiery end in the Great Fire of London in 1666. The cathedral had been a place where booksellers could store their books, but these caught fire and destroyed the cathedral. On 14 May 1675, Charles approved Wren's plans and construction began.

Construction work was not as straightforward as one might imagine. Although it was opened during the reign of Queen Anne in 1708, it was by no means finished. The creation of the cathedral ultimately spanned the reigns of five monarchs, and finally was completed during the reign of King George. Various mason-contractors were hired, including Thomas Strong, Joshua Marshall, Edward Pearce and Edward Strong, among others. Master Baroque woodcarver Grinling Gibbons created the decorative features on the organ. The interiors of the cathedral were entrusted to James Thornhill, who also created the interior of the Painted Hall in the Old Royal Naval College, Greenwich. Approximately £1 million were spent in the construction of the new St Paul's – a massive sum in the Stuart period!

As more and more modern skyscrapers begin to dwarf Wren's Cathedral, it is fascinating and humbling to think of the fact that this cathedral dominated London's skyline for over 200 years. It is humbling to think that such great beauty of architecture could have been made before modern technology, before computers, before Health and Safety – some might say they did a better job than modern architects. St Paul's is one of the most beloved buildings in the United Kingdom. Its mathematical beauty, so carefully designed by Wren, has stood tall and strong against many obstacles, including when it was bombed during the Blitz in 1940.

33. The Stuart Era Had the First Poets Laureate

The Stuart era had some of the greatest poetry in history. With great poets such as William Shakespeare, John Donne, Andrew Marvell, William Congreve, Matthew Prior, it's hard to find better. A Poet Laureate is a poet who is appointed by a monarch into a post in which the poet writes poems in honour of major national events or royal celebrations, generally a birth, birthday, wedding, etc. Traditionally, this position was to last for the poet's lifetime, but in the late 1990s this was changed to only last ten years. The office of Poet Laureate often went together with the position of Historiographer Royal.

Although some claim Ben Jonson (1572–1637) and Sir William Davenant (1606–68) were the first of the Poets Laureate, the first *official* holder of the prestigious position was John Dryden in 1668. Born in the small village of Aldwinckle in Northamptonshire, England, in 1631, Dryden eventually went to Cambridge University and then became one of the most talented poets and playwrights of the seventeenth century. Although he found work as a poet during the Interregnum, Dryden was really a Royalist, and his true nature was revealed in the panegyric *Astraea Redux*, in honour of the Restoration in 1660. *Absalom and Achitophel*, arguably Dryden's most well remembered poem, controversially satirised various members of Charles II's court, skilfully turning Charles into King David, Charles's illegitimate son the Duke of Monmouth into Absalom and Shaftesbury as Achitophel.

Dryden was also a prolific translator of classical literature, including Homer's *Iliad*, Virgil's *Georgics* and *Aeneid*, Horace's *Odes*, Ovid's *Metamorphoses* and works from later writers such as Boccaccio and Chaucer. As for his plays, Dryden wrote several, including *All For Love* from 1678, which was based on Shakespeare's Antony and Cleopatra. In this play, Dryden's Cleopatra states, 'My love's a noble madness ... But I have loved with such transcendent passion, I soared, at first, quite out of reason's view, and now am lost above it.' Dryden's position under Charles II and then Charles's successor James II was generally pleasant enough, but that changed in 1688.

Seventeenth-century Britain was not hospitable to Catholics, and especially after the revolution of 1688, Dryden – as a Catholic – soon found himself in an uncomfortable situation. He was ultimately given the boot when he refused to pledge loyalty to the new Protestant sovereigns, William and Mary. Dryden worked with English composer Henry Purcell, who didn't seem to mind that Dryden was no longer in their good books. When Dryden died in 1700, William III was still on the throne, although by that time he ruled alone. Taking Dryden's place in 1689 was one Thomas Shadwell. Following Shadwell's sudden death in November of 1692, Nahum Tate was appointed.

Neither Tate nor Shadwell made as great an impact on the world of poetry as Dryden had. Indeed, Dryden was later revered by several poets in the nineteenth century. The Romantic historical novelist and poet Sir Walter Scott was such a fan that he compiled *The Works of John Dryden*, in 1808.

34. The Greenwich Observatory Was Created to Solve the Longitude Problem

A popular destination for tourists, the Greenwich Observatory sits atop the highest elevated land of Greenwich Park, which overlooks Greenwich Village, the Queen's House, the Old Royal Naval College and, just beyond that, the mighty River Thames. Inside the Observatory hang two large portraits. One is of King Charles II, under whose command the building began, and the other is of his brother, James II. The Observatory is important for a variety of reasons, not least the fact that it houses one of the best observatories in the world, one that was created to solve a very tricky problem.

One of the biggest scientific problems that faced the Stuart age was that of longitude. Charles II's warrant to create the Observatory stated that its aim was to 'find the so-much desired longitude of places, for perfecting the art of navigation'. It was proposed that in order to accurately determine longitude, an intense study of the stars was crucial.

On 22 June 1675, John Flamsteed was given the position of Astronomer Royal. This was the first time anyone had been given this position, and while Flamsteed was paid £100 per annum, the twenty-nine year-old apparently had to pay for many instruments himself (no doubt much to his annoyance). Christopher Wren designed the Flamsteed House, and Robert Hooke was involved in the construction. Flamsteed had a rather antagonistic relationship with Isaac Newton, who by some accounts was not a very nice fellow.

The Scilly Naval Disaster of 1707 proved without a doubt how important creating accurate navigation was for seamen. On the way back from a mission in the Mediterranean, the British ships ran into some very nasty weather, and because they weren't able to accurately measure longitude, the ships ran into rocks on the south-western part of the Scilly Isles. Considered one of the worst maritime disasters in British history, it left over 2,000 men dead, including Sir Cloudesley Shovell, and several ships destroyed. With so many lives lost, and potentially many more at stake, Queen Anne's government passed the Longitude Act in 1714, which was an 'Act for providing a Publick Reward for such Person or Persons as shall discover the Longitude at Sea'.

After over forty years in the position of Astronomer Royal, John Flamsteed died in 1719, without having been able to solve the problem that had been the reason behind building the observatory in the first place. His death paved the way for the next man to hold the post, his former assistant Edmond Halley – the man now best known for Halley's Comet. By this, time, of course, the Stuart era had ended, following Queen Anne's death in 1714. Despite great efforts by many of the brightest minds of the Stuart era, the discovery of longitude ultimately belongs to the Georgian period. John Harrison (born in 1693) was not an astronomer but a brilliant clockmaker, whose invention finally made it possible to determine longitude at sea.

35. Monmouth's Rebellion Ended at the Battle of Sedgemoor

Within months of James II's accession to the throne in early 1685, his nephew James Scott, Duke of Monmouth, left his exile on the Continent and sailed to England. Thus began the ill-fated Monmouth Rebellion, in which the popular, Protestant Duke of Monmouth invaded England in order to take the throne away from his uncle, the Catholic King James II. On board his ship were eighty-odd followers, a truly pitiful number for a rebellion, but Monmouth was certain that all Englishmen would rise up and join him against his uncle. The rebellion lasted a little over a month, but with poorly trained and armed rebels Sedgemoor was the area in which Charles II's eldest illegitimate son, the Duke of Monmouth, led one last attempt to beat James II's army.

Outnumbered by better-trained and better-equipped royalist soldiers, Monmouth's ragtag army had little chance. Monmouth, a seasoned general, knew the limitations of his rebel army well enough and so had few options. He and Lord Grey climbed the Church of St Mary, Bridgwater, and surveyed the enemy encampment. The tower that these men climbed is now known as Monmouth's Tower. As an experienced military leader, Monmouth knew that his cause only had one last chance and that was a night attack. They muffled their horses' hooves and made their way to the encampment, narrowly missing patrolling dragoons. Suddenly shots were fired, their cover was blown and the Battle of Sedgemoor had just begun. What followed was little less than carnage. Although there have been many wars since 1685, the Battle of

Sedgemoor remains one of the last pitched battles to take place on English soil.

Monmouth and several other rebel leaders fled the bloody field but with a £5,000 reward on his head, he was soon caught and punished. Forde, Lord Grey, Monmouth's friend, got off lightly after he wrote a full confession. Those who weren't killed on the battlefield were rounded up and marched into a nearby church in Westonzoyland. Some were summarily executed. Some died of their wounds inside the church. The rest faced trial at the Bloody Assizes, presided over by the notorious 'Hanging Judge' Jeffreys. Some were executed, some 'transported' – meaning sent over to New World colonies pretty much as slaves, while others were severely fined. Monmouth, even though he was King James's nephew, had a very bad end on Tower Hill. He had one of the worst botched executions in history.

36. The Duke of Monmouth Was Dashing, but Doomed

The man who became known as James Scott, Duke of Monmouth and Buccleuch, was born on 9 April 1649, in Rotterdam. His mother was a beautiful Welsh Royalist exile, Lucy Walter (or Barlow), and his father was none other than the exiled King Charles II. Although there is debate as to whether or not his parents were married, Monmouth was in all probability illegitimate. James Crofts, as he then was known, had a difficult upbringing in which his father eventually had him kidnapped from his mother, who died in impoverished circumstances.

Charles indulged his son and the boy proved a poor student, failing to grasp basic writing and mathematics until his teens. Monmouth had some spectacularly nasty aspects to his personality. He was prone to violence upon the slightest provocation or perceived slight against him or his father. In time, however, he became a talented and capable military leader. When he was fourteen, his father married him off to the twelve-year-old Scottish heiress, Lady Anna Scott, Duchess of Buccleuch, and together they had several children. The extraordinarily handsome Monmouth was a libertine and notoriously unfaithful to his wife. His most notable mistress at one time was Eleanor Needham, with whom he had two children. In the decade that preceded his death, however, Monmouth fell in love with Lady Henrietta Wentworth; she became his last mistress and the great love of his life.

Monmouth's continual involvement in political intrigues led to his exile, and William and Mary received him at their court in the Dutch Republic.

Upon hearing of his father's death in early 1685, he was persuaded by fellow exiles to take his father's throne, which had by then passed to his uncle, King James II. Monmouth's Rebellion was disastrous. Monmouth, fleeing from the Battle of Sedgemoor, was eventually caught near Ringwood and hauled to London where he was imprisoned in the Tower of London.

On 15 July 1685, he was taken from his cell in the Bell Tower and up to Tower Hill, where he ascended the scaffold and gave the executioner a bag of money. This was standard practice in order to hopefully be killed quickly and as painlessly as possible. Unfortunately, the executioner was Jack Ketch, the man who had badly botched the beheading of William, Lord Russell, back in 1683. The thirty-six-year-old rebel leader knelt and laid his head on the block and suffered five strikes of the axe, which still did not sever his head, forcing Ketch to finish him off with a knife. Monmouth's execution has as a result gone down as one of the most horrific executions in Tower history.

Following his death, his mutilated corpse was taken back into the Tower and he was interred in the Chapel of St. Peter ad Vincula, by the wall behind the altar. Those buried near him include Anne Boleyn and Katherine Howard – Henry VIII's beheaded wives. James Scott, Duke of Monmouth, remains one of the most tragic, popular and romantic figures of the Stuart period.

37. The Stuarts Had Some Pretty Normal Hobbies

The Stuarts enjoyed a variety of pastimes and hobbies, some which you have probably enjoyed at some point yourself. The Stuart family were very athletic and so sports were a popular pastime among them. Mary Queen of Scots was apparently quite keen on golf, it being a Scottish invention. Her grandson, Henry Frederick, Prince of Wales, was a keen horse rider. He also enjoyed swimming, which seems to have been the cause of his death as he decided to go swimming in the notoriously dirty River Thames and some water got into his mouth.

Charles II had a boundless amount of energy and he was known for walking very quickly and often. He also enjoyed playing bowls and tennis, something that he had in common with his younger brother Henry, Duke of Gloucester, who was very skilled at playing the game. He liked the game so much, he had Henry VIII's tennis court at Hampton Court Palace done up and used it regularly. Charles and his other brother, James, were interested in horseracing and would often go up to Newmarket for these. The theatre was also a source of great diversion for the Stuarts and they both went to the playhouses and had private performances at their palaces.

Charles II also loved sailing and is credited with making yachting a popular hobby, and his favourite yacht was called *Jemmy* – the same name he gave to his son James, Duke of Monmouth. Dancing was another popular pastime, and one which most Stuart family members were good at. The Duke of Monmouth was an exceptionally good dancer, and Pepys commented once that he was always leaping about and full of energy.

Mary II was also an accomplished dancer and an excellent walker. William III loved hunting because it gave him an outlet for stress and plenty of exercise and the fresh air that his asthmatic lungs so badly needed. His sister-in-law Anne also loved hunting and riding, but in later years her extreme poor health meant she had to hunt in a carriage.

However, not all hobbies were so active. Among the more cerebral, there were hobbies that included scientific experiments (Rupert of the Rhine was particularly keen on these) and looking up at the heavens through a telescope. This was a great time of discovery, and these people were fascinated by it all. William III also loved collecting art, something that his grandfather Charles I had enjoyed very much as well. Mary II was crazy about collecting blue and white china. She also enjoyed more sedentary pursuits, such as embroidery and cards. There is a beautiful screen in Mary II's bedroom in Het Loo Palace in the Netherlands, which was embroidered by Mary and her ladies-in-waiting. Anne had a good ear for music and had guitar lessons when she was growing up.

Even though these people lived over 300 years ago, it's nice to know that they enjoyed the same kind of hobbies that we still enjoy today.

38. Not All Members of the Stuart Family Were Buried Together

Westminster Abbey contains the tombs of many royals dating all the way back to the early 600s. The most well known Stuart tomb is that of Mary Queen of Scots. Although she was originally buried in Peterborough Cathedral following her execution in 1587, her son James VI/I had her reburied here once he came to the English throne. He also had a marvellous marble effigy created to top her grave and it remains a beautiful monument. James himself is buried in the Abbey along with his wife, Anne of Denmark.

Many of the second most famous Stuarts are buried in the Stuart vault in King Henry VII's Lady Chapel. Within the vault, Charles II's tall coffin is by the wall and next to him rests his niece, Queen Mary II; beside her lies her husband, King William III, then Anne's Prince consort, Prince George of Denmark, followed lastly by Queen Anne herself. In another vault in the Abbey rest Henry Frederick, Prince of Wales (d. 1612), Arabella Stuart (d. 1615), two infant children of Charles I and Henrietta Maria, Elizabeth Stuart (the Winter Queen/Queen of Bohemia, d. 1662) and her son Rupert of the Rhine (d. 1683). Henry Stuart, Duke of Gloucester, younger brother to Charles II and James II who died from smallpox in 1660, also rests with them, as does Anne Hyde (d. 1671) and several of her children with James, Duke of York.

Not all of the most well-known Stuarts were buried in the Abbey, however. Following his execution on a cold day in late January 1649, Charles I's corpse and his severed head were sent to Windsor. The former king's body was then taken to St. George's Chapel in

Windsor Castle, where his body was cleaned and his head stitched back onto his body (pity the person who was entrusted with that job!). With almost none of the Christian burial rites he would no doubt have wanted, he was buried in the same vault, which also houses the remains of King Henry VIII and his third queen, Jane Seymour. Visitors to St. George's Chapel can walk over the ledger stone, upon which is carved the names and dates of the bodies that lie in the vault below.

Charles's grandson, the Duke of Monmouth, is also not buried in Westminster Abbey due to the fact that he was executed for being a traitor, and so is buried in the Chapel of St. Peter ad Vincula in the Tower of London. Monmouth's son with his wife Anna Scott, however – James Scott, Earl of Dalkeith, who became a well-respected soldier. When he died in 1705, he was buried in the Abbey.

Three Stuarts were laid to rest in France. Henrietta Maria, queen of England, was buried in the Basilique Royale de Saint-Denis along with her youngest daughter, Princess Henrietta (Minette). King James II, who as a result of being overthrown in 1688, lived in exile in France and was buried at the Chapel of Saint-Germain, but his tomb – along with the tombs of many other royals – was sadly destroyed during the many horrors of the French Revolution.

39. John Milton Was Blind and Impoverished When He Died

John Milton was one of the most important poets of the seventeenth century, and with his *Paradise Lost*, he remains one of the most important figures in English literature. Born in London's Bread Street in 1608, Milton grew up to become a fervent republican (anti-monarchist) and a strong critic of church clergy, especially Archbishop Laud. He was educated at Cambridge University, from which he received two degrees. His personal life was controversial, for he wrote several pamphlets in favour of divorce and this was received with hostility. Milton was married three times and had three daughters from his first marriage.

During the English Civil Wars, he was a staunch supporter of Parliament; when the monarchy was abolished and Cromwell took the role of Lord Protector, as Cromwell's secretary, Milton was considered to be his right-hand man. Milton was a brilliant propagandist. When the popular pro-Stuart propaganda *Eikon Basilike* was released just days after Charles I's execution, Parliament had their work cut out for them. *Eikon Basilike* very much made Charles I into a martyr, and indeed he is referred by some as the Martyr-King. Milton was countered with *Eikonoklastes*, his 1649 Parliamentarian propaganda piece. It simply didn't beat the emotional impact of the *Eikon Basilike*, but Milton fared better in his *Defensio* two years later.

He also wrote *Areopagitica,* which was *A Speech for the Liberty of Unlicensed Printing to the Parliament of England*. In this monumentally important polemical tract, Milton opposed licensing and censorship of books, writing, 'It will be primely to the discouragement of all learning, and the stop of truth, not only by disexercising and blunting our abilities in what we know already, but by hindering and cropping the discovery that might be yet further made in religious and civil wisdom.' It was an early defence of free speech. His prose is elegant and often powerful – 'He who destroys a good book kills reason itself.'

Fortunes rise and fall, and the pendulum of politics is a notoriously fickle mistress. With Cromwell's death and the subsequent dissolution of the Republic, Milton soon found himself losing nearly everything. To say he was unhappy to see the return of kingship to the Three Kingdoms would be an understatement. Upon the Restoration, those who had been favoured under the Republic found themselves vilified under the new order. Milton's radical views were complete anathema to those of the Restoration. Courtier and diarist John Evelyn interceded on Milton's behalf, and that may well be the reason why Milton did not face prison time or worse.

One of Milton's most moving poems is unquestionably his *When My Light is Spent* – in this poignant poem, Milton lamented the increasing loss of his eyesight. In 1667, his destitution meant he had to sell his copyright to *Paradise Lost*, for which he received a measly £10. When he died in 1674, completely blind and living in poverty, it was a pitiful end for such a talented individual. As is the fate for most writers, Milton came to more recognition posthumously.

40. Most of Whitehall Palace Was Destroyed by Fire in 1698

Whitehall Palace was one of the most important palaces in British history. Originally York Place, it was a residence for archbishops. When Cardinal Wolsey's power was on its descent, Henry VIII took possession of the sprawling palace for himself. Since then, Whitehall had become the main base from which monarchs would attend to affairs of state. It was at Whitehall Palace on 28 January 1547 that Henry VIII died. It was at Whitehall that his daughter Elizabeth promenaded with her 'Frog', the Francis, Duke of Anjou during negotiations for a possible marriage between them in 1581. And it was in the Star Chamber where Mary Queen of Scots was declared guilty. Whitehall Palace was also where Elizabeth gave her Golden Speech to members of the Commons in 1601. It was also here that one of the most shocking events in British history occurred, when Charles I was publicly beheaded outside the Banqueting House. Whitehall also served as the site where Charles II made a speech at the Restoration.

All this history came to a fiery end when a terrible inferno broke out in 1698. According to reports from the time, a careless maidservant left clothing to dry by a fireplace, which caught fire and quickly spread throughout the palace. The majority of the sprawling Tudor complex was destroyed, with the exception of the Banqueting House, which is a magnificent building in itself and boasts one of the most beautifully painted – and strongly symbolical – ceilings in the world. It was here that foreign ambassadors had been received and masques had once been performed. During Elizabeth

I's reign, three banqueting houses were constructed. The Banqueting House itself was designed by Inigo Jones, following its predecessor's destruction by fire in 1619. Jones was deeply influenced by the architecture he had seen abroad, and he incorporated features such as Ionic columns; it was constructed between 1619 and 1622.

Also lost in the 1698 blaze was the Whitehall Mural by Hans Holbein the Younger, depicting Henry VII, Elizabeth of York, Henry VIII, and his third wife, Jane Seymour. Fortunately for us, however, Remigius van Leemput painted a small copy of the mural in 1667 during the reign of Charles II. A portion of Holbein's original cartoon (large drawing or study) was happily not destroyed and is on display at the National Portrait Gallery in London.

This hadn't been the first time a fire had broken out at Whitehall during William's reign. In 1691, the Stone Gallery and the Duchess of Portsmouth's apartments had caught fire. Following the second (and most destructive) inferno, King William III – who by then was ruling alone, his wife having been dead for four years– had it turned into a Royal Chapel. It largely remained a chapel until late into the reign of Queen Victoria, at which point it was turned into the Royal United Services Museum. In the late twentieth century, that museum was removed and it ultimately became looked after by the charitable organisation Historic Royal Palaces, which looks after it and several other castles and palaces.

41. James II's Followers Were Known as the Jacobites

King James II, openly and devoutly Catholic in a time when Catholics were regarded with fear, suspicion, and hatred, was an unpopular monarch by the time he ascended the throne in 1685. As he was the legitimate king, however, there were those who supported him, particularly following his exile in 1688. These followers were known as Jacobites (from the Latin *Jacobus* = *Jacob* = *James*). There were three major Jacobite periods – one directly following the Glorious Revolution of 1688, the 1715 uprising, and finally the 1745. Those who supported the Protestant cause with William III of Orange were known as the Williamites. Whig history has been particularly kind to the Glorious Revolution, and this interpretation has come under severe criticism from revisionist historians in the twentieth and twenty-first centuries.

When King James II, 'The King Over the Water', died – still in exile – in 1701, his son James Francis Edward Stuart became King James III, a fact ignored by everyone except his father's loyal supporters, the Jacobites. It was by no means certain that a Protestant succession would continue, and some important members of William III's and Anne's courts kept the communication channels open with the exiled royals. Pamphlets, including *Seasonable queries relating to the birth and birthright of a certain person*, from 1714, brought up some pertinent questions. From a completely neutral view of the situation, the young prince really had been denied his birthright.

On 1 August 1714, Queen Anne died and the throne passed to another branch of royals descended from James I – the Hanoverians (also known as the Georgians). There was no question of Anne's half-brother James Francis Edward getting a chance at the throne, for he was a staunch Catholic. John Erskine, 6th Earl of Mar, led the Jacobite Rising of 1715 but the Georgian army defeated this rebellion.

James Francis Edward married the Polish noblewoman Maria Clementina Sobieski, who was a granddaughter of the Polish hero Jan Sobieski III (of Battle of Vienna fame). The couple had two sons, Charles Edward and Henry Benedict. The latter became a Cardinal in the Roman Catholic Church, but the former became the leader of the Jacobite rebellion of 1745 and was known as The Young Pretender', and, more famously, Bonnie Prince Charlie. The Jacobites fought against King George II's army and were defeated at the Battle of Culloden on 16 April 1746. The Jacobite defeat resulted not only in the loss of many men, but it even destroyed the culture of the Scottish Highlands. Why? The Scots, in particular the Highlanders, were largely Jacobite. In the year following this final pro-Stuart rebellion, George II's government issued the Act of Proscription, in which traditional Highland dress (tartans, kilts, etc.) was banned.

Even though over 300 years have passed since the revolution overthrew James II in 1688, some of the more radical modern-day Jacobites do not regard the current monarch of the United Kingdom as legitimate because they only count the line of those who have directly descended from James II and Mary of Modena.

42. Kensington Palace Became a Royal Residence in the Late Stuart Period

Now the home of the Duke and Duchess of Cambridge and their family, Kensington Palace wasn't always a royal abode. Kensington was once a sleepy, verdant village outside of London and renowned for its purity of air. Royals have only inhabited the house since the late seventeenth century, when William III and Mary II moved in. A Jacobean house was built in 1605 for Sir George Coppin, three years after an earlier Neyt Manor structure was razed. Following Coppin's death in 1619, it was purchased by the Finch family. Much later on, the house was named 'Nottingham House' because Sir Heneage Finch was the Earl of Nottingham (since 1681).

In 1688, what is known as the Glorious Revolution occurred, in which James II was ousted from power by his nephew and son-in-law, William of Orange, and James's daughter and William's wife and cousin, Mary. In 1689, William and Mary were crowned King and Queen, and they soon set out to find where to live. Why? You may well wonder, considering that they already had St James's Palace and Whitehall Palace. But Whitehall rested in an area by the River Thames that was full of fog, smoke, and generally unpleasant air. This wreaked havoc with King William's chronic asthma and so more verdant climes were sought. They soon purchased Nottingham House from Daniel Finch, the 2nd Earl of Nottingham (who happened to be his Secretary of State), for a whopping £14,000–18,000.

After this, they hired Sir Christopher Wren to expand and modernise the Jacobean building into something bigger and more fashionable. Construction work went on between 1689–90. Unfortunately, Mary was a bit impatient with what she perceived to be the slow progress of the building. This can probably be attributed to her desire to make a comfortable home for William. Her over-eagerness to get the building works completed meant that the workman built too quickly, and so the quality of their work became a secondary consideration. As a result of this, November 1689 saw part of the newly built building fall down, 'killing seven or eight workman' – this tragedy also occurred during renovation work to Hampton Court Palace.

The gardens were redone at this time as well, with heavily manicured box hedging elaborately formed in the formal Baroque (modern) style, which was then so popular. William and Mary spent nearly the same amount on these magnificent gardens as they did on the house! They both loved gardening and their previous homes in the Dutch Republic (the Netherlands), especially Paleis Het Loo, also had wonderfully symmetrical parterres in this elegant style. In 1690, the interior of the house began to be decorated with glorious woodcarvings from Baroque carver Grinling Gibbons. Outside the Queen's Entrance, the monogram of William and Mary is clearly visible above the doorway.

William and Mary's felicity was but short-lived, for Mary died in December 1694. William died eight years later in 1702, at which point Anne became queen. Her greatest contribution to Kensington Palace was the Orangery, which was designed by Hawksmoor and Vanbrugh and built in 1704–5.

43. Some Stuart Ladies Had Killer Beauty Regimes

Lady Venetia Stanley was one of the most celebrated beauties of her day. Married to Kenelm Digby and widely admired, one can suppose she tried everything within her power to maintain that great beauty once the effects of age began to take their toll. One of the things she used was viper wine – a wine which had viper venom mixed into it. Sir Kenelm Digby went into her bedchamber one morning and found her dead – but in such a state as to make her seem as though she was only asleep. The distraught widower had the great Flemish Baroque painter Anthony van Dyck paint her on her deathbed. Van Dyck also created another sumptuous posthumous portrait of Lady Digby between 1633 and 1634.

While it has never been proven that the viper wine killed Venetia, Lady Digby, many ladies – especially in the early part of the Stuart era and earlier than that in the Elizabethan age – could die from their makeup. White porcelain skin was very much desired in the Early Modern era, and women who didn't naturally have the shade would resort to sometimes-deadly means of obtaining it. Lead-based cosmetics, particularly ceruse, were used to paint the skin white and lead poisoning did occur. Over time, such makeup eventually had damaging effects upon the skin. Some makeup contained arsenic and mercury! Deadly nightshade (*Atropa belladonna*), an extremely toxic herbaceous plant, was used since ancient times as a cosmetic. During the Stuart era, some women continued to use this potentially deadly plant in eye drops to make their eyes shine beautifully.

44. Sir Christopher Wren Was the Man

He was an architect, scientist, inventor, astronomer and mathematician. Nearly everything Christopher Michael Wren put his hand to was done well. Even his contemporaries highly esteemed him; John Evelyn called Wren 'an incomparable genius'. Born in Wiltshire, England, in 1632, he was just a boy when the civil war broke out, and his father was the Dean of Windsor. His uncle, Matthew Wren, Bishop of Ely, was imprisoned in the Tower of London for eighteen years until the Restoration.

Wren enjoyed an excellent formal education and attended the University of Oxford, from which he obtained his MA. Later on, he became Professor of Astronomy at Gresham College. Wren was also one of the founding members of the Royal Society – an institution that continues to this day. In 1661, Wren was the top astronomer in the country when he was appointed Savilian Professor of Astronomy. This was a huge boost to his career. Like most of his colleagues, Wren attempted to solve the problem of longitude, but was unsuccessful. With the use of a telescope, Wren observed Saturn and the moon.

As an architect, he left us some truly masterful works of architecture, including St Paul's Cathedral, the Old Royal Naval College in Greenwich and the Monument to the Great Fire of London. Post-Fire London saw the erection of fifty-one new churches designed by Wren. His work was heavily influenced by the architecture designed by the Italian Baroque architect Bernini, and Wren was very pleased to meet him when he travelled to Paris in 1665. Bernini's work at the Vatican and the Louvre speak for themselves, and it's no wonder that

Wren drew inspiration from them. By the end of his life, London was very much Wren's London.

A man of his time, he enjoyed frequenting coffeehouses. Wren was also a family man. His first wife, Faith, gave birth to two sons but died from smallpox in 1675. His surviving son with Faith, Christopher Wren Jr, would later compile information about his father and family, which was published as *Parentalia*. In 1677, Wren married his second wife Jane Fitzwilliam, who bore him another two children before she too died in 1680 from tuberculosis. He never remarried.

By the time of his death in 1723 at the then very old age of ninety-one, Wren had already firmly put his stamp on the world and upon London's skyline. He was laid to rest in St Paul's Cathedral – arguably his greatest architectural achievement. His tomb has the fitting epitaph, 'If you seek his monument, look about you.' Few people in history achieved as much as Wren did in his lifetime, and that's why he was *The Man*.

45. Cromwell Was King in All but Name

From gleefully being the third signature on Charles I's death warrant to becoming the most powerful man in the Three Kingdoms, Lord Protector Oliver Cromwell was unquestionably a king in all but name. A descendent of Thomas Cromwell's sister, Oliver may have refused the crown when it was offered to him in 1657, but by having taken the position of Lord Protector, the regicide (killer of Charles I) took up residence in the former king's palaces, including Whitehall Palace and Hampton Court Palace. Both palaces were refurbished and remodelled to an extent. In the latter, Cromwell had his apartments decorated with mythological tapestries and paintings. He and his wife would walk around with their own retinues.

Cromwell also demanded that everyone refer to him as 'His Highness', and his family became a de-facto royal family. His favourite daughter, Bettie, was indulged as if she were a princess. Her wedding was like that of a royal wedding and at her death she was buried in Westminster Abbey. Privately, Cromwell enjoyed music and had a small staff of musicians. This may come across as rather strange, given how church music during the Interregnum had been prohibited and church organs destroyed.

Not everyone was pleased with the decidedly royal direction Cromwell began to take. Cromwell had his personal security boosted by hiring highly paid bodyguards. This was because Cromwell realistically could have been assassinated. Several assassination attempts were made, including by former Leveller Colonel Sexby.

Cromwell died of natural causes in Whitehall Palace

in 1658 and his body was embalmed – the way a king's body would have been prepared. After lying in state at Somerset House, he was given a state funeral and interred at Westminster Abbey – again, like a king. His son, Richard Cromwell, succeeded him in the same hereditary manner. But with Cromwell's death, so died the Republic. Richard – rather cruelly nicknamed 'Tumbledown Dick' – was nothing like his father and his position of power soon came to an end. Eventually, General Monk marched the army into London and in this coup, the Republic was firmly shut down and the return of the king was called for.

At the Restoration of the monarchy in 1660, King Charles II ordered Cromwell's body to be disinterred from its resting place in Westminster Abbey and posthumously hanged and beheaded. His embalmed head was mounted on a spike and appears to have still been up there until the time of the Rye House Plot in 1683. An embalmed head purported to be Cromwell's was a source of controversy in the nineteenth and twentieth centuries, and was eventually buried in Cromwell's alma mater, Cambridge University, in 1960. And what of Cromwell's legacy? For centuries people either loved him or hated him, but like any human being, he was complex. What is amazing about Cromwell is that he rose up from the gentry, became Lieutenant-General of Horse in the New Model Army, laid siege to several towns, expelled the Rump Parliament, and finally became the Lord Protector.

46. Ireland Often Got a Raw Deal

Since Tudor times, English Protestants had settled Ireland in what were called plantations. In the early 1600s, there was the Flight of the Earls and their lands were then taken and more colonists moved in. In 1641, Irish men and women rose up against their English colonisers in what's known as the Ulster Uprising of 1641, which only added to King Charles I's many problems. Irish Catholics massacred Protestants and vice versa, and the situation was pretty bad for about a decade.

Lord Protector Cromwell was particularly vicious in his treatment of the Irish and still has a very poor reputation throughout the Emerald Isle. Cromwell's reputation remains decidedly unpopular, for during the Third English Civil War and then the subsequent Cromwellian regime, Ireland suffered greatly. In early Autumn 1649, Cromwell invaded Ireland, and in September launched an attack on Drogheda, which had been taken before by the Royalist-Confederate Catholics. What ensued there came to be known as the Massacre of Drogheda. He also had people butchered in Wexford. Over 2,000 people were killed.

When Charles II was restored to the throne in 1660, the lands that were taken away under Cromwell weren't returned. The Irish were let down once again. By the late 1680s, Ireland still had a majority Catholic population and so many supported James II. Loyalty to James meant that Ireland was eventually on the losing side during the Glorious Revolution of 1688. Following Williamite and Jacobite skirmishes around the country, and then solid defeats at the Battles of the Boyne and Aughrim, some Irish ended up calling James II *Séamus an Chaca*, or 'James the Shit'. The Irish Jacobites were not without heroes. Patrick Sarsfield, Earl of Lucan, was a brave leader who was eventually fatally shot at the Battle of Neerwinden (Landen) in 1693.

If economic and political turmoil weren't bad enough, Ireland also got its share of pestilence. Plague was a problem throughout Europe, but it swept through the Emerald Isle in 1604–5 and again in 1650–1. As a consequence of the Glorious Revolution, Londonderry and Dundalk had major outbreaks of Typhus and Dysentery. Thousands of people died. The controversial Orange order and Orangemen Parades in present-day Northern Ireland have their roots in the late Stuart age, for they are named after King William III. William was also the Prince of Orange (hence the 'orange') and is credited with liberating Irish protestants from Papish tyranny and giving them religious freedom. The annual parades commemorate Wiliam's decisive victory over James II at the Battle of the Boyne in 1690. So from disease to colonisation, warfare, and unfortunate political situations, Ireland often got a raw deal.

47. The English Civil Wars Changed Everything

The Wars of the Three Kingdoms have been given so many names – the English Civil Wars, The Great Rebellion, the British Civil Wars – but no matter what you choose to call this tumultuous series of wars, one thing is certain: they changed everything. Either directly or indirectly, the wars affected all aspects of society and people all across the kingdoms. The English Civil Wars were three different wars over the years 1642 to 1651. This was by no means the first civil war in England. There were several, the most important of these being The Anarchy in the twelfth century and the Wars of the Roses in the fifteenth century.

Popular culture and even some textbooks have perpetuated many myths about the civil war of the seventeenth century. A case in point is this belief that Royalists (Cavaliers) were made up of only the well-dressed rich snobs and the Parliamentarians (Roundheads) were the hard-working people. The reality was much more complex. Seven years of conflict ensued, in which whole families were torn apart, first perhaps by differing views, and then by the violence of war. Wales usually goes unmentioned because it is so closely associated with England, but Wales played an important role because it was largely in support of Charles I.

The First English Civil War period contained several important battles. The Battle of Edgehill is notable because it was the first major battle of the civil wars. The Battle of Marston Moor in July 1644 was a decisive win for the Parliamentarians, who had few casualties compared with the Royalists. The Battle of Naseby in Northamptonshire is unquestionably one of the most important and decisive battles in British history. In mid-June 1645, the three-hour battle between the Royalists led by Prince Rupert and the New Model Army led by Sir Fairfax ended again in the slaughter of the Royalist army. The victorious Parliamentarians then turned their attentions to the over 100 women in the Royalist camp – thinking these were Irish (they were probably Welsh) they were killed, raped, or disfigured.

The Second English Civil War was the shortest of the three wars. While the fighting took place in 1648 there were important events that took place from 1647 to 1649. In 1648, General Fairfax led the Parliamentarians to besiege and defeat the Royalists at Colchester. In December of the same year, Colonel Thomas Pride forcibly removed all MPs who were against trying the king (among other things). This was known as 'Pride's Purge' and it culminated in the establishment of the Rump Parliament and the trial and execution of Charles I in 1649.

In the Third English Civil War, Royalist forces attempted to invade England from Scotland with Charles II, who was made King of Scotland in 1651. The Battle of Worcester was the last battle of the civil wars and brought all Royalist hopes to a crashing end. Charles was only just whisked away from the battlefield in time and he hid in a hollow of an oak tree near Boscobel House. Scars from the English Civil Wars can still be seen throughout the country. Birmingham's Aston Hall, for example, has a wooden main staircase that still bears the damage it sustained from a cannonball.

Once the fighting was over, everything had changed – even the monarchy was impacted and would never again be as it was before the civil wars.

48. Masques Were a Formal Entertainment, but Some Thought Them Immoral

Masques were a formal entertainment, and they were rather like a play with music. They were extravagant, costly productions that required elaborate costumes and spectacular sets, and were performed at night lit by torchlight. They were truly magical events, and to be able to witness them was pretty special. Masques were very popular during the sixteenth and seventeenth centuries, but really came into their own during the early Stuart age, in which they were not only entertainment but also propaganda pieces. Ben Jonson, one of the most popular playwrights of his time and a contemporary of Shakespeare's, often collaborated with Inigo Jones to create these masques (Jonson and Jones squabbled frequently!). If the costume designs from Ben Jonson's *The Masque of Queens* are anything to go by, this meant that some of the women performed bare-breasted.

Henry Frederick, Prince of Wales, that paragon of princely virtues, enjoyed masques as well, so they couldn't have been very explicit. In 1610, Henry commissioned Jonson to write a masque, which was performed the following year and entitled *Oberon the Fairy Prince*, with the prince himself in the title role. Inigo Jones's costume designs for this masque are sumptuous combinations of ancient Roman and Renaissance styles. Henry's mother, Anne of Denmark, was an enthusiastic commissioner and performer in masques as well.

Queen Henrietta Maria was particularly fond of performing in masques – and this was met with disapproval by those, particularly certain clergymen, who thought women performing in such spectacles were immoral. To the most radical puritans, masques were in their very nature evil. Militant Puritan pamphleteer William Prynne wrote the scathingly critical and controversial *Histriomastix: The Player's Scourge, or Actor's Tragedy* in 1632, and this was seen by some as a direct attack on the queen. Indeed, Prynne's writings in this come across as no more than the angry and vicious ranting of a religious zealot. 'These so vain, so pernicious, so sacrilegious plays and spectacles are to be avoided of all Christians.' Throughout the work, he continues his attack, stating, 'The subject matter of stage plays is oftentimes impious, sacrilegious, blasphemous,' and that plays directly contribute to 'the fomentation of diverse lusts'.

As late as 1675, John Crowne's masque *Calisto* was performed at Whitehall Palace before Charles II and Catherine of Braganza. The players in this production included the future queens Mary II, as the titular heroine Calisto, and Anne. Other performers included the Duke of Monmouth and Nell Gwynn. This last person was a popular actress. We tend to take actresses for granted now, but there was a time when it was illegal for a woman to perform on a public stage. It was Gwynn's royal lover, King Charles II, who allowed women to act in public. As his own mother had acted in masques earlier in the century, it is not very surprising that the monarch allowed this. However, there remains debate as to who was the first actress to appear on stage – it seems likely that Margaret 'Peg' Hughes was the first, following her performance as Desdemona in Shakespeare's *Othello* in 1661.

49. Stuart Philosophers Ushered In an Age of Reason

The philosophy of the seventeenth century is unquestionably important, especially when one considers that the philosophical works from this era paved the way for the Enlightenment thinking of the eighteenth century. Ideas spread, and so we have to look at the whole of Europe in this fact. In France, philosophy began to take interesting directions under great thinkers such as Rene Descartes (of 'I think, therefore I am' fame) and Blaise Pascal (notable for Pascal's Wager). In England, Francis Bacon (1561–1626) and Thomas Hobbes were some of the most influential thinkers of the early Stuart era.

Francis Bacon, from whom we get the term 'Baconian', died when he developed pneumonia after conducting an experiment in the snow. Thomas Hobbes made a significant impact on modern philosophy as well. The term 'Hobbesian' refers to men's lives, without laws or a power to keep them in line, as 'solitary, poor, nasty, brutish, and short'. In other words, we need to be ruled because that is in our best interest. Hobbes was thoroughly admired during the Stuart period, and biographer John Aubrey wrote one of his longest and most detailed biographical entries for him.

The impact of Locke's philosophy is readily apparent to those who have read both his writings and the Constitution of the Unites States of America. Locke voyaged across from the Dutch Republic to England when William and Mary took the throne in 1689, and he was a staunch supporter of their reign. His works, including *An Essay Concerning Human Understanding* as well as his *Two Treatises of*

Government, were two of the most influential on the Founding Fathers.

The Stuart era as a whole was a period in history in which people seemed to have been frightened and confused. I say this because, on the one hand, they were thoroughly entrenched in superstition and deeply religious, but on the other hand, scientific endeavour was beginning to take off. In that century, we had the likes of Galileo, Newton, Leibniz, Cassini, Descartes and many others seeking answers to some of mankind's greatest questions. To have such great leaps in science and industry while simultaneously maintaining religious and superstitious beliefs must have been difficult for some people.

50. William and Mary Didn't Manage to Modernise All of Hampton Court Palace

Lying by the River Thames approximately 12 miles south of London, Hampton Court Palace remains a breath-taking sight. The building that greets visitors is largely a palace of two halves – the newer Baroque version, built by William and Mary in the late seventeenth and early eighteenth centuries, and the older Tudor building, in which Cardinal Wolsey, Henry VIII, Anne Boleyn, and later Elizabeth I lived.

When they came to the throne officially in 1689, William and Mary went house hunting because the foul conditions at Whitehall Palace severely aggravated William's asthma. More verdant climes were sought, and they purchased what came to be known as Kensington Palace. Hampton Court Palace, Windsor Castle and St. James's Palace were already theirs by right of being the sovereigns. Hampton Court, by that time, was a sprawling Tudor building ; it was well over a hundred years old and considered very old-fashioned. The rooms were damp and so in order to make it habitable, some modernisation was needed. William and Mary's uncle, King Charles II, had added a few improvements, including the Long Water.

William and Mary decided that they would have most of the antiquated Tudor palace knocked down to make way for a modern, Baroque palace – a palace, William hoped, to rival Louis XIV's extravagant Versailles in France. The only thing that was to be kept from the Tudor building was the Great Hall. A good deal of the palace was demolished and a new design created by master architect Sir Christopher Wren. Demolition of the old Tudor building and work on the new began in 1689, and in the interim, Mary set up temporary apartments in the old Water Gallery. This she had filled with her favourite blue-and-white china and the newly made series of portraits of the Hampton Court Beauties.

William and Mary hired Jean Tijou and Daniel Marot, two French Huguenots, to decorate the new part of the palace. Tijou's exceptionally beautiful Baroque wrought-iron screens are still located at the far end of the Privy Garden. Marot was an architect and furniture designer specialising in the ultra-modern Baroque style. Master Baroque woodcarver Grinling Gibbons was also employed to carve wooden decorations throughout the King's and Queen's Apartments.

In December of 1694, Mary II died suddenly from smallpox. A grief-stricken King William III had construction stopped for around three years; after all, the money had started to run out. Unlike his French rival across the sea, William's purse was held by Parliament and his costly wars against the French meant that the full-scale plan of modernisation had to be stopped. In 1697, the widower was doing better politically (the Peace of Rijswijk had just been signed) and financially, and had construction work continue on Hampton Court Palace. During this time, he had the Little Banqueting House built and commissioned Antonio Verrio to decorate the interior of this and the main apartments, most notably the King's Staircase and the King's Little Bedchamber.

51. Pirates, Especially the Barbary Pirates, Were a Constant Terror

Forget jolly pirates with a penchant for imbibing rum. Real pirates were no joke; they were brutal. Piracy has been a problem for centuries (even Julius Caesar was captured by pirates!), and is a problem seafaring vessels face even now in the twenty-first century. During the Stuart era, pirates were a cause for great concern – especially those known as the Barbary Pirates. The Barbary States referred to the coastal areas of North Africa, comprised of the modern-day countries of Morocco, Libya, Tunisia, and Algeria. When King Charles II married the Portuguese Princess Catherine of Braganza, part of her dowry included the port towns of Bombay (modern-day Mumbai, India) and Tangiers. The latter, however, proved to be a hub of piratical trouble. Surviving political documents from the time suggests that successive reigns had a pirate problem.

In 1631, Barbary pirates attacked the village of Baltimore in Ireland. Barbary pirates were known for landing the coasts of England, Wales, Scotland, and Ireland, where they would capture European men and women and take them to Algiers to be sold. The former were either killed or forced to work the galleys on ships; the latter were usually sold off as sex slaves in harems. The National Archives in Kew contain reports that state how some English officials were taken prisoner and held for ransom.

By the time of the Restoration in 1660, it was Charles II's turn to deal with pirates; he and the Sultan of the Ottoman Empire endeavoured to tackle the problem. In article XIX, page 7, of *The Capitulations and Articles of peace between the Majestie of the King of England and the Sultan of the Ottoman Empire* from 1663, it says, 'If the pyrates or Levents who infest the seas with their frigates, shall be found to have taken any English vessel, or to have robbed or spoiled their goods, & faculties ... our ministers shall seek out such offenders & severely punish them, and cause that all such goods, ships, monies, and whatsoever ... be presently, swiftly, and absolutely restored to them.' Whether or not that worked is impossible to tell. Page 2 of Issue 14 of the *London Gazette* for 16 May 1670 states that 'the pyrates of Algier have taken three Portugal ships bound for Brasile'.

The Barbary Pirates were by no means the only pirates on the seas, and others were just as menacing. English pirate John Ward was the most notorious pirate of the late sixteenth and early seventeenth centuries, and was so infamous that several ballads were written about him. Captain Kidd was hanged in London in 1701, and his body was kept in an iron cage as a warning to others not to go into piracy. However, the Golden Age of piracy was by then in full swing. Daniel Defoe wrote *A General History of Pyrates*; in this, he stated that it was dangerous for 'governments to be negligent, and not take an early care in suppressing these sea bandits before they gather strength'.

52. Boys Wore Skirts Until 'Breeched'; Women Sometimes Dressed like Men

In many portraits of young aristocratic families during the Stuart period, it can appear as though there are no boys; even the toddlers are wearing skirts or dresses. This would be because it was customary for boys to wear skirts, much like girls, until they were 'breeched' or given their first pair of breeches. This was a symbolic event, showing that they were moving from the world of being looked after by women and towards becoming men, and would usually take place between the ages of six and eight. After the Stuart era, this age grew younger and younger until the tradition stopped.

There are many portraits from the Restoration on that depict aristocratic women wearing men's clothing. The two most famous paintings that feature this include the Simon Verelst portrait of Mary of Modena, *c.* 1675 and Simon Cooper portrait of Frances Stuart from the mid-1660s. In both, each lady is wearing a male periwig and cravat – both of which were thoroughly masculine. Stuart, in the buff coat, has the plainer outfit of the two, as Mary of Modena's appears heavily embroidered. Trends come and go, and in this period of Stuart history, it was the height of fashion for women in the highest echelons of society to wear masculine attire when out hunting or riding. The rest of the time it really wasn't the done thing to dress like a man, but some women did anyway, such as Hortense Mancini and Queen Christina of Sweden. These ladies usually did whatever they wanted anyway.

53. Daniel Defoe Kept Getting into Hot Water

Daniel Defoe, or De Foe (*c.* 1660–1731), is now only remembered for his popular and exciting novels. *A Journal of a Plague Year* follows one man's experiences through life during the plague outbreak of 1665. *Robinson Crusoe*, a tale of the sole survivor of a shipwreck, is a well-loved children's adventure classic. *Moll Flanders* and *Roxana* were remarkable, for Defoe wrote from a fallen woman's perspective. What most people don't know is that he ran into a lot of trouble during his seventy-odd years on Earth.

Born in London, and prohibited from attending a university because he was of a Dissenting family, Defoe nevertheless received a good education from Morton's Academy in the Stoke Newington area. When he was still a young man, Defoe joined the Monmouth Rebellion of 1685 as a rebel. It wasn't all he thought it would be, and when King James II issued a Royal Pardon a few weeks later, he took advantage of it and left (thus sparing himself the horrors of the Battle of Sedgemoor and the Bloody Assizes). He must have believed there was something in Monmouth's claims of legitimacy, because later on he wrote a pamphlet on the possibility of a succession through Monmouth's children.

Throughout his lifetime he was plagued by serious financial troubles, which landed him in prison a couple more times. Defoe moved around quite a bit (being chased by his creditors could have had something to do with this). He rented a house in Stoke Newington and then leased a house in Colchester, Essex. He is also believed to have lived in Tooting (then known as

Tooting Graveney) at some point. Oddly enough, for someone with a consistently poor track record when it came to personal finances, he wrote about economics several times!

Not one to let past troubles get in his way, Defoe became a political pamphleteer. A staunch supporter of William and Mary and the Glorious Revolution that had placed them on the throne, Defoe wasn't the type to sit idly by when other writers began attacking William because he was a foreigner. Defoe hit back at William's critics with the hugely popular *The True-Born Englishman: A Satire* of 1701. During the reign of Queen Anne, Defoe was placed in a pillory as punishment for seditious pamphleteering. There, instead of having rotten food (or worse) thrown at him, he was pelted with flowers.

Once the Georgians were on the throne, he faced another problem; some people accused him of supporting the Jacobites. This he vehemently denied in the 1715 pamphlet, *Appeal to Honour and Justice,* in which he wrote, 'No man in this nation ever had a more riveted aversion to the Pretender and to all the family he pretended to come of, than I; a man that had been in arms under the Duke of Monmouth, against the cruelty and arbitrary government of his pretended father; that for twenty years had to my utmost opposed him (King James II) and his party after his abdication.'

54. Stuart Gardens Were Baroque-Tastic

The early Stuart period was known as the Jacobean period, and during this time gardens shifted from the popular knot gardens of the Tudor age to more practical Jacobean gardens. These gardens weren't completely about aesthetics, as many gardens contained herbs which would were used to treat a variety of physical ailments. There were also kitchen gardens, in which vegetables were grown for the preparation of food. One of the most well-preserved Jacobean gardens (and houses, for that matter) is Chastleton House, near Moreton-in-Marsh in Oxfordshire.

Most fashions throughout the seventeenth century came largely from France, and the French fashion for elaborate formal gardens was no exception. The French influence upon gardens stems from the highly popular gardens at Versailles, with their ornate formal parterres. Earlier in the seventeenth century, in the Dutch Republic, the exotic tulip set off a craze known as 'Tulip Mania'. In this spectacular example of an early economic bubble, a single tulip bulb was worth a stupendous amount of money. But when the bubble burst, a tulip bulb became worthless. A similar fate did not happen to pineapples, but they were used as status symbols. The first pineapple grown in England was presented to King Charles II by the royal gardener, Mr Rose. The late 1670s painting *Charles II Presented with a Pineapple*, which is in the Royal Collection, depicts this scene.

France had some competition, however, in their great enemy the Dutch. The most important aspects of Late Stuart gardens are symmetry, formality, and beauty. Box (*Buxus sempervirens*) was one of the most commonly used hedges for Baroque gardens as it was easy to trim. Geometric shapes played a major role in these types of gardens and one usually sees conical-shaped topiaries in such a design. Sometimes animal figures were created from the topiaries. These heavily manicured gardens required an immense amount of maintenance.

During William and Mary's reign, Kensington Palace's gardens were updated to this new Baroque type of garden, but in a Dutch style, which was not as ostentatious as the French. The maze at Hampton Court Palace, so often misattributed to Henry VIII's time, was an addition made during William III's reign (1689–1702). Mazes, as well as fountains, were a popular feature in Baroque gardens. Mary was an avid collector of both blue-and-white porcelain and exotic plants. The latter was shipped over following her and William's rise to power in 1689 and a greenhouse/orangery was constructed at Hampton Court Palace to accommodate these plants.

Notable examples of Baroque gardens include the recently renovated gardens at Paleis Het Loo in The Netherlands. Het Loo was one of the homes built for William and Mary in the late seventeenth century. In England, the Privy Garden of William III is as it would have looked back in 1702. Baroque gardens were often found at some of the grandest homes. At Chatsworth House, the first Duke of Devonshire had variety of Baroque structures added to his gardens, such as the Cascade and the Cascade House.

55. There Were More Plots in the Stuart Era than in a Soap Opera

And that's not a good thing! From the Gunpowder Plot in 1605 to the Rye House Plot in 1683, there were many plots, scandals and intrigues in between. The Overbury Poisoning Scandal ruined Robert Carr's position as favourite to King James I. Lady Frances, Countess of Somerset was young and gorgeous and already married to the 3rd Earl of Essex. This marriage was annulled on the grounds of not being consummated, leaving Frances free to marry again. Overbury was a poet and Robert's friend and he didn't like Frances, and this compelled him to write the poem 'A Wife'. It was an obvious attack on Frances and she was one ticked-off woman. She plotted to get him incarcerated in the Tower and there she had him poisoned over a period of time. When Overbury died, everyone assumed it had been of natural causes. Francis married Robert, and somehow the poisoning element got out and the couple were found guilty and sentenced to death, though the king commuted this sentence to imprisonment in the Tower.

The Popish Plot in the late 1670s was an elaborate conspiracy theory maliciously concocted by Titus Oates and Israel Tonge that stated that there was a plot by the Catholics, to assassinate Charles II. When Sir Edmund Berry Godfrey, the magistrate looking into Oates' and Tonge's allegations, was found dead in a ditch, his own sword sticking out of his body, it whipped people up into an anti-Catholic frenzy. Edward Coleman was a secretary for the Duke and Duchess of York and he was one of several (probably innocent) men who were accused of and executed for treason. Catherine of Braganza, the queen herself, was accused of being privy to the plans to assassinate her husband.

The Rye House Plot of 1683 soon followed the Popish Plot. This plot was to assassinate King Charles II and his brother, James, Duke of York (later James II) on their way back from the racing at Newmarket. They were to be set upon at one of the toll stops and assassinated, opening the way for a truly Protestant succession, with the Duke of Monmouth likely becoming king. This plot followed hard upon the Exclusion Crisis, which began in the late 1670s and was spurred on by fears that Charles's eventual death would lead to his Catholic brother James, Duke of York, becoming king. The Exclusion Bill to prevent James from coming to the throne was led predominantly by Anthony Ashley Cooper, the 1st Earl of Shaftesbury. Several notable figures of the day were implicated in the Rye House Plot, including the Duke of Monmouth and Lord Russell. The latter was subjected to execution by beheading, which was lamentably carried out by the soon-to-be-notorious Jack Ketch, who bungled it, requiring three chops of the axe before Russell's head was severed from his body. Under William and Mary, Russell was given a posthumous pardon – much good that did him!

56. We Really Can't Blame a Mole for William III's Death

There are a number of myths that have sprung up about the Late Stuarts, more so than about the earlier ones. One of these is that William III was instantly killed in a horse riding accident. While King William III did die following an accident, the real culprit was plain old pneumonia. William's lungs were already in a poor state as he had suffered from chronic asthma throughout his life. On 21 February 1702, the king went for a ride out on Home Park at Hampton Court Palace. There, his horse stumbled upon a molehill, which threw the king off violently, whereupon he landed on the ground and broke his collarbone. This was the reason why many Jacobites toasted to the 'little gentleman in the black velvet waistcoat' (the mole).

After his broken collar bone had been set, he demanded to be taken to Kensington Palace, which is approximately 12 miles away from Hampton Court Palace and where he had a meeting scheduled with his ministers that evening. The carriage ride there was bone-jolting, and William must have been in great pain because the bone had to be re-set upon arrival at Kensington. After this, he took a few turns around what is now The King's Gallery and sat down and fell asleep by an open window (it was a cold February day), which overlooked the elegant parterres of his Baroque gardens. His fall was not especially bad; his injuries were not life-threatening, and after all, this was a man who had sustained musket-ball grazes and the like upon his many experiences upon the battlefields of Europe.

William awoke feverish and feeling ill (no surprise

there, falling asleep in front of an icy draught!). Over the next few days his condition deteriorated, but he was able to continue to work and hold meetings with his advisors. Soon enough, however, it became clear that the king was at death's door. His favourite, Arnold Joost Van Keppel, was by his side when he became very ill in March. At this point, the King asked for his old friend Hans Bentinck, with whom he had fallen out a few years earlier. Bentinck arrived shortly before William breathed his last – 'Je tire vers ma fin,' or 'I draw towards my end.'

And so, William Henry, Prince of Orange, Stadtholder of the Dutch Republic, and King of England, Scotland and Ireland died on 8 March, 1702, around eight or nine o'clock in the morning. As he had been born in November of 1650, he was only fifty-one years old. The post-mortem examination, which was carried out by a group of eminent physicians (including Dr Bidloo and Dr Richardson), revealed the broken bone was in the process of healing (and therefore not the cause of death), but the lungs displayed clear evidence of pneumonia; it was that which killed the king, not a mole! William's coffin was placed beside that of his wife, Mary II, in a vault in Westminster Abbey.

57. Dogs Were Popular with Kings and Kitchen Staff Alike

It is often said that a dog is a man's best friend, and indeed, traditional British culture has an inherently strong love for the animal. This was pretty much the case in Stuart Britain. The royals of the Stuart era were very fond of dogs – Charles II was known for his many spaniels (which came to be known as King Charles Cavalier spaniels), and William and Mary for their pugs. Mary II loved her dog, True, so much that upon his death she had the poet Matthew Prior compose a poem in his honour. Prior did write a poem and entitled it *An Epitaph on True, Her Majesty's Dog*. Dogs accompanied their masters on the hunt, and they are often seen in portraits of the aristocracy. The most popular seen in Stuart portraits include breeds such as the papillon, poodle, maltese, whippet, greyhound, spaniel, and pug.

Most high-tech Stuart kitchens needed a dog to function. These dogs would run on a wheel contraption that would turn the spit so that roasts could cook evenly without a person having to manually turn the spit. That being said, dogs weren't always looked upon so kindly. There was dog-fighting, which, like cock-fighting, pitted dog against dog while humans stood around cheering and placing bets. During the Great Plague, however, thousands of dogs (and cats) were killed in order to prevent further spread of the dreadful disease. They were also susceptible to intestinal worms that could pass to humans. Bigger dogs, such as mastiffs, were useful as guard dogs, while other dogs were used as food for other animals, such as hawks.

58. The 2nd Duke of Buckingham Duelled over a Married Woman … and Won

George Villiers, 2nd Duke of Buckingham, was one of the most debauched of the Restoration rakes. As the son of the murdered first Duke of Buckingham and the rich heiress Katherine Manners, he was born into privilege and elite social rank. This was, however, of short duration for the English Civil Wars thrust him and his younger brother, Francis, into war. Francis was killed in battle, and eventually George and other Royalists like him had no choice but to flee the country and go into exile.

As soon as the Restoration began, Villiers soon married Mary Fairfax – the daughter of the major Parliamentarian leader, Sir Thomas Fairfax. Villiers' interesting choice of wife (she was considered plain) – and the fact that her father consented – is surprising. Sadly for his wife, it was not long before Villiers started to indulge in extramarital affairs, and one of these liaisons was with an already married woman; a woman who developed a reputation for being a *femme fatale*.

Countess Anna Maria, wife of Francis Talbot, 11th Earl of Shrewsbury, was a very beautiful woman who was considerably younger than her husband. Once married to Shrewsbury, the French-born beauty soon had several Restoration rakes buzzing around her like bees to honey, including the notorious rakes Henry Jermyn and Harry Killigrew. Anna Maria's flirtatious manner with the various would-be lovers didn't help matters, and some very crude poems were written about her and Jermyn. When the handsome and dashing George Villiers, 2nd Duke of Buckingham, began his pursuit of the countess, Anna Maria was unable to resist his charms and their adulterous union began. The two lovers were not very good at keeping their amour clandestine. Indeed, they were quite open about the whole thing and the affair was on the lips of everyone at court. Unsurprisingly, Anna Maria's husband couldn't stomach being made a cuckold – especially in so public a manner. Understandably enraged and dishonoured, the Earl of Shaftesbury demanded a duel with the Duke of Buckingham in 1668.

In an ironic twist of fate, George ended up killing Francis in the duel, and the newly widowed Anna Maria moved in with George and his wife! Mary was shocked and dismayed by the unwelcome addition of her husband's shameless mistress into their marital home, and when she protested against it, Buckingham was believed to have told her he could send her (his wife) back to her father instead! From this point, they lived in a presumably awkward ménage-a-trois. Anna Maria gave birth to Buckingham's son, who died soon after. A few years later, Buckingham tired of Anna Maria and he died in miserable circumstances, alone. Anna Maria, on the other hand, her reputation long having been in tatters, went into a convent but then married again. No duels or scandals plagued this marriage, and she died in 1702. Charles Talbot, Anna Maria's son by her slain husband, became the much-respected 1st Duke of Shrewsbury, who served William III, Anne, and George I.

59. English Architecture Shifted from Late Renaissance to Exuberant Baroque

The Elizabethan style of Renaissance architecture led to the Jacobean style, which maintained many elements that typified the former. Some of the best examples of Elizabethan architecture are Longleat and Burghley House.

The next big change in English architecture began during the reign of Charles I, and this is often referred to as the English Palladian style. Andrea Palladio was a Venetian architect whose innovative designs were met with much admiration by fellow architects. One of these admirers was Inigo Jones, who designed the Queen's House in Greenwich and the Banqueting House in Whitehall. Kinross House in Scotland was built in 1685–6 and designed by Sir William Bruce in a neoclassical Palladian style. Bruce had previously been commissioned by King Charles II in the 1670s to rebuild the sixteenth-century Palace of Holyroodhouse near Edinburgh.

Jacobean architecture is known for a variety of features, including interestingly shaped gables and balustraded parapets. Ham House is a spectacular Stuart-era house in the leafy village of Ham, in Greater London. It was built in 1610 and went through some alterations in the 1630s, but is a remarkably very well-preserved example of Stuart architecture. This house was leased to William Murray, Charles I's friend who once was his whipping boy. This stately home is often used in films, including the 2000 television version of *Lorna Doone* and 2009's *The Young Victoria*.

Baroque architecture was generally more flamboyant than the styles previously mentioned. This style utilised decorative cornicing among other things, to present an impressive aesthetic. Perhaps the most astounding of all English Baroque buildings is Blenheim Palace, which was built for John Churchill, 1st Duke of Marlborough, in honour of his great military achievement at the Battle of Blenheim of 1704. Sarah Churchill, his wife, was so demanding that she caused the architect John Vanbrugh to quit! Vanbrugh's assistant Hawksmoor ended up completing the job alone. Chatsworth House in Derbyshire is another example of English Baroque architecture. The Baroque style was added to the existing Tudor building in 1696 under architect William Talman and for William Cavendish, 1st Duke of Devonshire.

Castle Howard in North Yorkshire belongs to that small but elite group of massive English Baroque architecture. Most famously used as the house in both television and film adaptations of Evelyn Waugh's *Brideshead Revisited* and the 1995 BBC mini-series *The Buccaneers*, this family home possesses a stunning dome and an elegant façade. Unfortunately, Castle Howard was badly damaged in a fire in 1940. The building was commissioned in 1699 by Charles Howard, 3rd Earl of Carlisle, and designed by Sir John Vanbrugh and Nicholas Hawksmoor.

In Northumberland, England, Sir John Vanbrugh designed Seaton Delaval Hall, again in the English Baroque style, in 1718. Hawksmoor's *c.* 1700 design for Easton Neston in Northamptonshire was another fine example of English Baroque architecture. Boughton House, also in Northamptonshire, has several features from the 1690s. English Baroque didn't last long, but there are plenty of examples to enjoy throughout the country.

60. Louis XIV of France Bankrolled Charles II of England

After nearly a decade on the throne, with greedy mistresses and the costliness of the second Anglo-Dutch war, King Charles II had a serious cash flow problem; like his father before him, he did not take kindly to having his purse restricted by Parliament. So when King Louis XIV of France offered a deal to him, he took it, although it was a very risky deal. Charles II of England and Louis XIV of France were first cousins, as Charles's mother and Louis's father were siblings. Family ties did not necessarily mean peace between their two countries, but wily Charles had a knack for diplomacy.

In return for the large amount of money (£200,000 per year and 6,000 troops) Louis was giving him, Charles would declare himself a Catholic and bring the Three Kingdoms under his power back to the Roman Catholic Church. Then, probably most importantly for Louis, Charles would have his military join together with that of France to crush the Dutch Republic once and for all. Never mind the fact that Charles was already in a Triple Alliance with the Dutch Republic and Sweden. It didn't matter that Charles's nephew, William of Orange, was not yet twenty years old and already prepared to die for his nation; Louis and Charles would keep him there in the semblance of a ruler. The idea was that they would rule through him. As history would eventually prove, both Charles and Louis completely underestimated the young Dutchman.

Louis sent his sister-in-law and Charles's youngest sister, Minette, over to take care of the treaty negotiations. The Treaty was signed in 1670, and only a handful of people knew about the secret clause. If word had got out of King Charles's commitment to bringing Catholicism back to England, there would no doubt have been a violent and terrible reaction of the blood-on-the-streets kind. The anti-Catholic hysteria, which came as a result of the fabricated Oates/Tonge Popish Plot later in the decade, proved just how explosive the Catholic issue was. Charles attempted to bring about a more religiously tolerant nation by introducing the second Declaration of Indulgence in 1672, but this proved unpopular. This hostility towards Catholics led to the Test Act of 1673, in which all government officials had to denounce transubstantiation – something Catholics would not be able to do, and so was used to exclude Catholics from office. Charles's brother, James, Duke of York, was a Catholic and so resigned his position in order to avoid having to take the oath.

Charles had always had a sort of soft spot for Catholics, which was evident at certain times in his reign. After all, his mother Henrietta Maria had been a devout Catholic, and his brother James was as well. On Charles's deathbed in 1685, he converted to Catholicism, thus keeping his word to Louis but also perhaps finally being true to his true beliefs.

61. The Stuart Period Had Some Truly Heavy-Handed Laws

For those who like law and order, the Stuart period had some strong measures to prevent and punish criminal behaviour. Depending on the crime, punishment was expected to include one or a mix of the following: time in the pillory (a pillory was similar to the stocks and used to inflict public humiliation on the offender), flogging/whipping, a stint in prison, transportation to the New World colonies or the death penalty. Debt could land you in a debtor's prison, such as the Marshalsea in Southwark or the Fleet. Thieves were usually hanged. Murder could land you in Newgate Prison and then executed. Prisons at this time were largely dreadful, pestilence-riddled places.

Traitors were subjected to the full force of the law. Usually following some kind of torture, the criminal would then be drawn on a sled to the place of execution, where he'd be hanged until he passed out. Then he would be awakened for the horrifically painful ordeal of having his entrails burnt in front of him, his genitals and then his head cut off. Traitors' heads would be mounted on poles or spikes in grim warning to others of the fate that would befall them too should they embark on a treacherous path.

Wealthy heiresses were often targeted for abduction and forced marriage and so the law frowned upon anyone who attempted such a thing. Major party-boy John Wilmot, 2nd Earl of Rochester, had his eye on the young and very wealthy heiress Elizabeth Malet. He was on the right track to marrying her legitimately, but he decided to abduct her anyway in 1665. He messed up and things didn't go according to plan.

Soon enough he found himself in serious trouble, and was thrown into the Tower of London. He eventually did get to marry Elizabeth, but not before sending grovelling apologies to King Charles II for his bad behaviour. He got off lightly. Some would have fared much worse.

There were some harsh punishments for seditious libel. William Prynne was an outspoken critic of Archbishop William Laud and of women performing, as in masques. He was pilloried, his ears cut off, and his cheeks branded with a hot iron. This kind of mutilation was common for his crime. Fast-forward to October 1648, when the House of Commons heard a possible case for reparations for Prynne and the two other men who had been pilloried with him for their seditious writings, Burton and Foxley.

Not all heavy-handed laws involved punishing criminals or political and religious dissenters. In 1695/6, 'an Act for granting to His Majesty severall Rates or Duties upon Houses for making good the Deficiency of the clipped Money' was passed. Among the various clauses of this law included the infamous Window Tax – popularly referred to as 'Daylight Robbery' by many a London tour guide. In order to avoid paying high taxes, many people opted to brick up their windows, and if you look closely at architecture throughout London, you'll still be able to see this.

62. Mary, Princess Royal, Had a Mother-in-Law from Hell

Her name was Amalia van Solms-Braunfels. She was the formidable mother of young Mary's husband, William II of Orange, and the wife of Frederick Henry, Prince of Orange. Mary Stuart, Princess Royal of England, was very young (twelve) when she moved away from her parents, siblings, and country to the Dutch Republic. Her one ally would be her new husband, William. But this would change a few years later when William, aged twenty-four, contracted smallpox and died. Nineteen-year-old Mary was heavily pregnant at the time of her husband's death, and she gave birth to a son only a week later. Mary had done well by giving birth to the heir to the House of Orange-Nassau, and she chose to name the boy Charles, after her father and eldest brother.

Amalia, however, conscious of the tradition of the family, denied Mary this and the boy was named Willem Hendrik, (William Henry). An already-devastated Mary was understandably aggrieved by this and refused to attend her son's christening. Her only ally was her aunt Elizabeth of Bohemia. Amalia took the reins and young William was given a thorough, strict education and upbringing. His mother, upon the news of her brother's restoration to the throne of England, joyously left the Dutch Republic to join in the festivities. While in London she, like her husband a decade before her, contracted smallpox and died, aged only twenty-nine. Her ten-year-old son was left an orphan and made a Child of State. Domineering Amalia continued to play a strong role in his life until her death in 1675.

63. A Sovereign's Choice of Spouse Could Make or Break Them

When Mary Queen of Scots married Henry Stuart, Lord Darnley, many were left shaking their heads in disbelief. He excelled in all things superficial. Save for the birth of their only child and heir, James, the marriage was an unmitigated disaster. Darnley was an abusive drunkard whose general depravity led to his contracting syphilis. In 1567, the twenty-one-year-old was murdered and a huge explosion at his lodgings was meant to cover it up. Mary and Henry's son, James, grew up to be an awkward fellow. In 1589, he married Anne of Denmark, who was a frivolous spendthrift of a woman and a Catholic. Ultimately, she had little negative effect.

Charles I, when still Prince of Wales, had made a daring journey to Spain to woo the Spanish Infanta but that proved a disaster. Instead, he ended up marrying Henri IV of France's daughter, Henrietta Maria. Henrietta Maria was a hugely unpopular choice, for not only was she French, but she was a devout Catholic, and she didn't know her place (which, at that time, meant not to meddle in politics). Despite the initial frostiness of their relationship, Henrietta Maria eventually became a devoted wife to Charles. During the civil war, she was separated from her husband, who was beheaded in 1649. Twenty years later, Henrietta Maria died in 1669 from what is believed to have been an accidental overdose of the opiates she had been taking as painkillers.

Catherine of Braganza, Infanta of Portugal, was the doe-eyed, long-suffering consort of Charles II. The worst part about her was that she was, again, a

Catholic. The good things were that she was young, presumably fecund, and extremely wealthy. For a king perpetually running low on funds, she seemed a perfect candidate. As a result of Portugal's mighty colonial conquest and trading routs, Catherine's dowry was impressive: Bombay in India, the North African port of Tangiers, several hundred thousand pounds in money, and more. Her personal charms were not sufficient to keep Charles faithful, and she proved unable to give him an heir, but when it came down to the crunch and he had pressure to divorce her, he refused.

When Anne Hyde died from breast cancer in 1671, James, Duke of York spent little time as a widower. Most people had frowned on his marriage to Anne because she was a commoner, and common sense would have told him to look for a protestant princess. He soon began looking for his next duchess, but unfortunately for him, he once again chose a wholly unsuitable bride. Mary of Modena was an Italian princess, and a devout Catholic – so devout, in fact, that she had been planning on entering a nunnery. James was a Catholic himself, and for him to have chosen a Catholic bride was an antagonistic move on his part, especially as the country was increasingly Protestant. It would have been in his best interest to marry an English Protestant of high birth, and his marriage to Mary of Modena certainly did him no favours.

64. Insatiable Royal Mistress Barbara Palmer Courted Trouble

Barbara Palmer, née Villiers, Lady Castlemaine, was the most notorious of all of Charles II's mistresses; she had a volatile temper, meddled in politics, and was sexually voracious. Married to John Palmer, she became Charles's mistress in the course of his exile during the time of the English Republic. Barbara was considered extremely beautiful, and her many portraits suggest as much. One would imagine that being mistress to a highly sexed monarch would be enough to satiate a lady, but that was not the case with Barbara Palmer. She was a volatile vixen and in one particularly violent episode, she threatened to bash her baby's skull against the floor if Charles did not do what she wanted. John Evelyn referred to her as the 'curse of the nation'; Samuel Pepys, however, was so taken by her substantial physical charms that he didn't seem to mind her behaviour. Barbara infamously posed for Peter Lely as the Virgin Mary, with one of her illegitimate sons as the Baby Jesus. Barbara had a knack for courting trouble her whole life long.

Charles II's strong libido was not enough to satisfy Barbara, and she took several other lovers to her bed – including her cousin, John Churchill (who later became the 1st Duke of Marlborough). Charles even caught the two in Barbara's bedchamber. As an older woman, she married a much-younger rake, Robert Fielding, who spent a lot of her money. To make matters worse, it transpired that Fielding was already married, thus making their union bigamous! Barbara died in 1709, at the age of sixty-three.

65. Stuart-Era Music Could Be Political, but Was Always Beautiful

Orlando Gibbons, William Byrd, and Henry Lawes were three of the most popular early Stuart composers. Music throughout the Stuart era could be political, often based on propaganda, but this never detracted from the beauty of the pieces themselves. The early part of the seventeenth century retained some musical features typical of the Late Renaissance, including polyphony and a cappella. Some composers straddled the Renaissance and the Baroque, including Italian composer Claudio Monteverdi.

Thomas Tomkins's *These Distracted Times* is quite possibly the most perfect music to convey the extremely tumultuous period of the English Civil Wars. There is an inherent sadness to the music that encompasses suffering and loss. Tompkins composed music to go with the lines from II Samuel, 18:33 (KJV): 'When David heard that Absalom was slain he went up into his chamber over the gate and wept, my son, my son, O Absalom my son, would God I had died for thee!' When one considers how many sons were killed during the civil war, this piece is even more moving.

A military victory was a cause for some music. One year after the Duke of Monmouth was executed, following the disastrous Monmouth's Rebellion in 1685, King James II commissioned the Italian Baroque composer Giovanni Battista Vitali to compose an oratorio. This piece was entitled *L'ambitione debellata ovvero La Caduta di Monmouth*, or *Ambition eradicated or The Fall of Monmouth*. During the Glorious Revolution, the popular tune of *Lilliburlero* became a propaganda piece for the Williamites.

Music didn't only express political beliefs and victories, of course, but the very personal human emotions of lust, sorrow, joy and love. John Dowland's 'Come again, sweet love doth now invite' is quite an erotic song. We mustn't forget that most of the stately music written for kings and queens often went unheard by most people. For your average Stuart, music was enjoyed in local taverns and public areas where folksongs were sung. Some of these songs were quite bawdy ('Pox on you for a fop') and often told tales ('The Countryman's Joy') or gave advice ('Good Advice To Bachelors, How To Court & Obtain A Young Lass').

Sometimes a composer's music could be happier than the composer himself. Jeremiah Clarke, for instance, was an English Baroque composer who had one of the most tragic lives of his contemporaries. Clarke's most celebrated piece is 'March for the Prince of Denmark' (written for Queen Anne's husband, George, Prince of Denmark), often referred to as 'Trumpet Voluntary', and is often used in happy occasions – namely for weddings. Clarke sadly never married, and it is believed by some historians that he committed suicide stemmed from an unrequited love for a lady. He shot himself in the head in a churchyard and died on 1 December 1707.

66. England and Scotland Were Not Officially United until 1707

Scotland and England have not had the best of histories. For hundreds of years, the two countries were enemies. Before that, the Romans thought fit to put up a wall – Hadrian's Wall – to divide England from Scotland. The union between England and Scotland has been a source of considerable controversy ever since it began in the Stuart era. It is a highly contentious issue even now and the source of many a heated debate. When the Scottish King James VI became King of England in 1603, it wasn't until the Acts of Union in 1707, under his great-granddaughter Queen Anne, that the union became official. Indeed, the Acts were possibly the most important event of Anne's reign, 'That the Two Kingdoms of Scotland and England shall upon the first day of May next ensuing the date hereof and forever after be United into One Kingdom by the Name of Great Britain'.

Between 1603 and 1707, Scotland had been involved in the civil wars, the Interregnum, the Restoration, and then the Glorious Revolution (which created more turmoil as some Scots allied themselves with the ousted King James II, others with William III). It was as a result of the Jacobite rebellion in 1745/6 that Highland culture was cut down. The union of Scotland and England was unpopular with Scots, but there were also those who were vocally supportive of union. In 2014, Scotland held a referendum and voters sided to maintain the union. Even so, there are still vocal supporters of independence – which rather goes to show that even after 300 years, at least that hasn't changed.

67. There Were Several Popular How-To Books

In the seventeenth century, there were quite a few books dedicated to various topics. Gervase Markham (*c.* 1568–1637) was a poet and a prolific writer on a variety of topics ranging from horsemanship and archery to translations of Italian works. It may come as a surprise to learn that one of the most popular guides to running the home was written by a man. Markham, you see, had also written about all things domestic in *The English Housewife, Containing the Inward and Outward Virtues Which Ought to Be in a Complete Woman.* It contained information on everything from cosmetics and cookery, to distillations. Hannah Woolley wrote *A Gentlewoman's Companion* in 1675 and *The Accomplished Lady's Delight* in 1677. These works held an array of useful tips on how to run a home efficiently.

The Ladies Dictionary, Being a General Entertainment of the Fair-Sex, compiled by an unknown author by the initials N.H. and printed for John Dunton in 1694, is another how-to guide. An early kind of dictionary, this large book contains a wide variety of topics among which are brief biographical entries about historical figures, including Joan of Arc and mythological beings such as Hylas. The book also contains useful tips on how to sooth sore nipples and the 'joys and real comforts' of marriage. It even has some advice for women hoping to become a lady's waiting-gentlewoman.

Besides the fact that both Markham's and Woolley's treatments for plague seem rather ridiculous to us now, their works nevertheless shed much light on domestic preparations in the Stuart era. All of the books mentioned above are still the go-to sources for researchers.

68. Anne Hyde Was a Commoner Who Became the Mother of Queens

Anne Hyde was born in 1637 to Edward and Frances Hyde. Sir Edward Hyde, Earl of Clarendon, was a respected lawyer and Lord Chancellor for King Charles II during his exile. Clarendon is best remembered in history for having created 'Clarendon's Code' and for writing *The History of the Rebellion*, which is one of the most important accounts of the English Civil War.

A plain-looking woman, but possessed of a good mind, Clarendon's daughter later became a lady-in-waiting to Mary, Princess Royal of England and Princess of Orange. It was while she was in this position that she caught the eye of the randy James, Duke of York. Promises of marriage were made – promises he most likely didn't expect to keep – because he was a prince and she was little better than a servant. They soon embarked on a sexual relationship, which soon enough resulted in Anne becoming pregnant. Obviously, their secret fling could no longer be kept hidden and a full-on scandal broke out. James tried to back out of his promise, and some of his friends came forward to claim that they, too, had carnally known Anne Hyde. His mother, Henrietta Maria, and his sister, Mary, were furious with them both because – in their minds – Anne was decidedly inferior to him in every conceivable way. He was a prince, and as such, only a politically or economically advantageous match would have been acceptable. Charles, annoyed at his brother's folly, nevertheless forced him to make an honest woman of Anne.

James and Anne married, and the latter moved up the social ladder from commoner to aristocrat by becoming the Duchess of York – a position she fulfilled well. Anne soon gave birth to a son, but the child died soon after. Eventually, however, the Duchess of York gave birth to two daughters who would survive: Mary, in 1662, and Anne, in 1665. At the time of their births, there was little thought that these girls would eventually become queens. After all, Charles was still rather early into his marriage with Catherine of Braganza, and there was time for him to sire legitimate heirs as easily as he had begat his illegitimate children.

As the years went by, Anne grew fat – partially a hereditary trait, as her father the Earl of Clarendon had grown fat as well (and a propensity to put on weight would finally come to beleaguer both her daughters), but also perhaps due to a bit of emotional overeating as a result of James's constant philandering. James, much like his elder brother, was an unfaithful spouse, and his mistresses had borne him several illegitimate children. Anne's favourite daughter was Anne, who later became Queen Anne. Mary was James's favourite child. Near the end of her life, she converted to Catholicism. At the age of thirty-two she died from breast cancer on 31 March 1672; some of her last words were to her husband. 'Ah, Duke! Death is very terrible! Very terrible!'

69. Questioning a Monarch's Sexuality Was a Tactic Used to Discredit Them

It is interesting that every single Stuart monarch who came after the Glorious Revolution has been labelled either homosexual or bisexual. One has to wonder whether this is a mere coincidence or if Jacobite propaganda was the impetus. Indeed, questioning a monarch's sexuality was perceived as a very good way to discredit them. William III, his wife Mary II, and Mary's sister Anne have all been labelled homosexual. It is rather unfortunate that the topic of William III's sexuality has remained a source of political ammunition for those on either side of the debate.

While this remains a source of controversy among historians, the fact remains that there is no evidence that William III was homosexual, or even bisexual. William had a couple of close male friends, mainly Hans Bentinck and later Arnold Joost von Keppel. Following the Glorious Revolution, William's preference for choosing foreigners as his favourites instead of Englishmen was met with hostility and envy. The Jacobites, William's enemies, latched on to the idea that the usurper was a homosexual and many explicit Jacobite pamphlets were made to hurt his reputation. When Bentinck became aware of these rumours about William and Arnold Joost van Keppel, he wrote to him about his concerns. William replied, shocked, that he couldn't believe people would mistake his kindness towards the young man to be criminal (as homosexuality was at that time).

William was, compared with his uncles Charles II and James II, not a highly sexed man. He was also very private about his affairs, which included a very long-standing extramarital affair with Elizabeth Villiers – one of his wife's ladies-in-waiting. Indeed, it is the Villiers relationship, and Mary's response to it, which gives us reason to believe that William was probably not homosexual. Mary was grievously hurt when she discovered his affair with Betty, but she never seems to have been hurt or jealous of his relationships with either Bentinck or van Keppel. On her deathbed, Mary pleaded for William to break away from Betty for the sake of his immortal soul. If he had been sexually involved with men, Mary (as a very pious woman) would have begged him to stop such a lifestyle.

Lesbianism, unlike male homosexuality, was not illegal. Mary's perceived lesbianism stems from her effusive adolescent correspondence with her friend Frances Apsley, later Lady Bathhurst. Mary was an intensely passionate, ultra-feminine girl and she and Frances enjoyed role-playing. Once Mary was married to William, however, all that passion and love was centred on him alone. From what we can gather from her personal papers, Mary had a reasonable sex life with her husband.

Queen Anne's lesbianism is another popular myth. Supporters cite Sarah Churchill's memoirs as proof but they forget or ignore the context of those writings. By the time she put quill to paper, Sarah had fallen out with Anne and been replaced by her cousin Abigail Masham as the queen's favourite. Like William III and Mary II before her, there is no evidence to prove that Anne was anything but heterosexual.

70. The Levellers and Diggers Were Totally Radical

Although they may sound like modern rock bands, these socio-political groups comprised two of the most radical ideologies in Stuart Britain. The period of the English Civil Wars is often described as a time in which the 'world turned upside down', and as more fringe groups began to evolve, it's hard to disagree. As more and more people began to question the conditions in which they lived, new groups formed that aimed to address grievances. As with many other topics briefly discussed in this book, the Leveller ideology is too complex to explain in sufficient depth, but it was quite popular because it demanded radical change.

The Levellers believed in equality and suffrage for all men (with some exceptions). The most notable Levellers were Colonel Thomas Rainsborough and 'Freeborn' John Lilburne. The latter spent a large amount of his adulthood in prison. Eventually, Lilburne was at odds with the new republic as well and was imprisoned and exiled. By the end of his life, however, he had converted to Quakerism.

There were quite a few Levellers in the New Model Army because the movement's aims were in keeping with their views. The inherent popularity of the Leveller ideology didn't sit comfortably with Cromwell and his associates. Leveller momentum led to the Putney Debates of 1647. These debates were talks held at St Mary's Church in Putney, and there members of the New Model Army discussed the future of the nation and officers listened to the concerns and grievances of the common soldiers – many of whom were owed pay. One of the Levellers' main speakers was Colonel

Rainsborough, who said, 'I think that the poorest he that is in England hath a life to live as the greatest he.' Royalists murdered Rainsborough in 1648 (though some suspect Parliamentarian involvement as well).

The Levellers were increasingly a menace in Cromwell's eyes, and things soon took a decidedly violent turn. In April 1649, the Bishopsgate Mutiny saw members of Colonel Whalley's army resist orders to leave London' for this, fifteen were court-martialled and a few were sentenced to death, although Robert Lockier was the only one of them to be executed. That wasn't the end of it. In the Banbury Mutiny of the following month, soldiers from the New Model Army rose up against Cromwell but failed. On Cromwell's orders, the three leaders of the mutiny – James Thompson, Corporal Perkins and John Church – were executed by firing squad on 17 May 1649. All three were Levellers. Those who believe in the principles for which the Levellers stood commemorate the men's deaths annually on Levellers' Day.

The Diggers, who referred to themselves as the 'True Levellers' (so as not to be confused with the Levellers), were a Protestant Christian group founded by Gerrard Winstanley and were even more radical than the Levellers. They wanted to abolish the monarchy and wanted land to be communal (hence the 'diggers' name). However, by 1650, the Diggers as a group were largely finished.

71. A Portuguese Princess Made Tea-Drinking Fashionable in England

Princess Catalina da Braganza, known to us as Charles II's wife and queen consort, Catherine of Braganza, came to England with a fondness for drinking tea. Although a costly beverage, the custom was already popular among the nobility back in her native country of Portugal. When she first appeared before her husband for the first time, she was asked if there was anything she would like to drink following her long journey. When she replied that she would like a cup of tea, this was met with amusement and a glass of beer was suggested as a more suitable beverage. After all, beer was the most popular drink in the country. In time, however, the Queen's favourite beverage began to be consumed by other ladies at court. After all, the habits and fashions of queens were naturally emulated by everyone who could afford to do so. Soon enough, this expensive and exotic drink became fashionable among members of the upper echelons of society.

That being said, some coffeehouses – namely Garaway's – claimed to have sold tea as a drink a couple of years before Catherine even set foot on English soil. Tea was consumed black with some sugar. As fine and fragile tea sets were made, milk began to be poured into the cup first in order for it not to break when the boiling water was put it. Even though mugs and teacups have become stronger throughout the subsequent three hundred years, it is still considered correct practice to put the milk in the cup first.

Later on in the nineteenth century, Anna Russell, the 7th Duchess of Bedford, was credited with the custom of afternoon tea. (On that note, the Dukes of Bedford have lived in Woburn Abbey for a few hundred years; it contains some amazing sixteenth- and seventeenth-century artwork and was visited thrice by King Charles I). Eventually, when tea became more widely available, it became popular with all parts of society and eventually became the most popular non-alcoholic beverage in British culture. As we all know, it's always a good time for a cuppa.

72. Two Royal Sisters Fell Out over the Duke of Marlborough's Tempestuous Wife

An endless variety of things can cause an irreparable rift between siblings, but in the case of the two York sisters – Mary and Anne Stuart – the cause of their falling-out was largely down to one person. Sarah Churchill (née Jennings) was a tempestuous, manipulative lady, and the more docile Anne was quite malleable in Sarah's hands. The three girls had performed together in John Crowne's masque, *Calisto, or The Chaste Nymph*, in 1675. Anne and her elder sister Mary had had more than their fair share of childhood squabbles, as is sometimes, if not usually, the case with siblings. There were even jealous arguments about mutual friends, particularly Frances Apsley.

When Mary left England to live with William in the Dutch Republic, Anne grew closer to Sarah, who soon married John Churchill, a rising military figure. Anne and Sarah even used pet names for each other. Anne was Mrs Morley and Sarah was Mrs Freeman. In 1683, Anne married Prince George of Denmark – a marriage that would be both very happy but very tragic with regard to their children.

It was largely due to Sarah's influence that Anne left her father to support William of Orange. After her father's exile, Mary returned to England and found her sister was largely under Sarah's thumb. Later, when Anne rather uncharacteristically asked her sister, now the queen, for a higher stipend, Mary smelled a rat. Mary knew the idea was Sarah's, not Anne's. Mary, unwisely choosing to confront her sister about Sarah when Anne was recovering from a miscarriage, told her to break her friendship with Sarah. Anne stubbornly refused to acquiesce to Mary's demands, and the sisters fell out and never saw each other again.

As Mary lay dying from haemorrhagic smallpox in December of 1694, Anne tried to see her but was denied from doing so, either from Lady Derby or by William himself. Thus, the estranged Stuart sisters were never reconciled. When William died in 1702 and the throne passed to Anne, Sarah rose to even greater prominence and power. Following her husband's decisive victory at the Battle of Blenheim, a grateful Queen Anne gave her friends the Dukedom of Marlborough and the royal estate of Woodstock. There they built Blenheim Palace.

Unfortunately, Sarah's manner towards the queen was often rude and insulting. On one occasion, she nastily told Anne to 'be quiet!' and eventually the queen had finally had enough of being belittled by her so-called friend. They had a terrible argument and the woman who had been the cause of the strife between the royal sisters was finally removed from her position of power. Sarah's cousin, Abigail Masham, took Sarah's place as Anne's favourite until the last Stuart monarch's death in 1714. Sarah, vindictive to the end, perpetuated malicious rumours about Anne's sexuality, even though there was no basis for them. Things didn't end so well for Sarah, though; her beloved husband died two years after Queen Anne, and her hot-tempered attitude ultimately alienated her from most of her children.

73. Roundheads and Cavaliers Both Had Important Players

In war, there are important figures to be found on both sides. James Graham, 1st Marquess and 5th Earl of Montrose, remains one of the great romantic heroes of the Royalist side. Although he was a member of the Scottish Kirk and had signed the National Covenant in 1638, he was not an extremist and decided to support King Charles I. Following the Battle of Naseby, Montrose went into exile on the Continent. After the king's execution in 1649, Montrose loyally served Charles II and fought for him in the latter part of the War of the Three Kingdoms (third English Civil War). In April of 1650, Montrose's small army was defeated and he found his way to MacLeod, who sold him out for the hefty ransom. Without a trial, Montrose was executed by hanging. His body was then quartered, the pieces sent to various towns in Scotland as a warning to others and his head mounted on a spike, where it stayed for eleven years until the Restoration.

General Thomas Fairfax, Parliamentarian leader, is one of the few figures from the English Civil Wars to be respected on both sides of the fence. He famously refused to sign the death warrant of Charles I, and as he was one of the main men on the Parliamentary side, he certainly would have been under pressure to sign it. Fairfax did not attend the king's execution, but was at prayer. According to John Aubrey, Fairfax had some of his troops protect the Bodleian Library. In later years, Fairfax received Roger Dodsworth's collections of historical papers (Dodsworth was an English antiquarian) and donated these to the library. Leeds Castle played a big role during the English Civil

War, as it was a prison and arsenal and had the benefit of having its owner on the winning side – Culpepper supported Cromwell's Parliamentarians. The Battle of Maidstone of 1648 took place not far from the castle, in which you can see Lord Fairfax's doublet on display.

Edward Montagu, the 2nd Earl of Manchester, was a commander of parliamentary forces and was respected by both Parliamentarian and Royalist alike because of his disposition. As the Major-General of the Eastern Association Army, he fought at such battles as Marston Moor. Unhappy with the direction things were going, the more moderate Montagu fell out with Cromwell and had to resign his commission. In a dignified move, he quietly backed away from politics during the Interregnum and became a strong supporter of the Restoration. Charles II in return gave Montagu the position of Lord Chamberlain, and Montagu's sons the positions of Master of Horse. The 2nd Earl of Manchester died in 1671.

These are just some of the men who were important figures during the civil wars. Others included William Waller, the 1st Duke of Hamilton, Henry Ireton, and more. There were so many figures during this time that it's simply impossible to include them all here.

74. John Churchill, Duke of Marlborough, Was a Great Military Leader

John Churchill is unquestionably one of the greatest military leaders in British history. He understood the importance of discipline and preparation. Churchill's rise from a mere page to one of the most powerful men in the Late Stuart courts is astonishing.

We cannot omit the women in Churchill's life because three of them were integral to his success: his sister Arabella, his lover and cousin, Barbara Villiers, and his wife, Sarah. Arabella was the mistress of James, Duke of York. As such, she was able to get her brother the position of page in the York household. Barbara Villiers was King Charles II's mistress, and possessed a voracious sexual appetite. She took the handsome young Churchill into her bed, and an oft-told tale of Churchill's youth is of how he was caught in his cousin Barbara's bedchamber by the king. Instead of getting angry, the king laughed it off, claiming the young man needed to do it to get his bread. Indeed, beautiful Barbara gave Churchill £4,500, which he took and invested wisely. Sarah Jennings became Churchill's wife in 1678 and her friendship with Princess Anne (later Queen Anne) would eventually bring the couple into greater power and wealth than ever before.

In the summer of 1685, Churchill, Lord Feversham and the Duke of Grafton led the Royalist army on behalf of the king and firmly thrashed Monmouth's rebels throughout the West Country, before finally crushing them completely at the Battle of Sedgemoor. Three years later, another nephew, William of Orange, attacked James II's throne and was so popular that

James's army left to join up with the Dutchman. Churchill left as well, which was an unexpected sucker-punch to James.

The new King William III never really trusted Churchill, the turncoat. How could he? James had trusted him completely, only to be abandoned in his hour of need. William's wife and queen, Mary, trusted him so little that she had him thrown into the Tower of London.

Churchill's power declined during William and Mary's reign only to reach unprecedented heights during the reign of their successor, Anne. This is when Churchill really got rolling. William III had had a life-long mission to defeat Louis XIV, but never really managed to do it. When Charles II of Spain died childless in 1701, he named Philippe of Anjou as his successor. The prospect of a massive empire of French and Spanish territories (including New World land and trade) was hugely disconcerting. Louis claimed no such thing would happen, and William III warned everyone not to trust Louis's word. No one believed him and Louis invaded the Spanish Netherlands. The War of the Spanish Succession had broken out and would last until 1714. Churchill teamed up with Prince Eugene of Savoy and the Dutch Republic to form the Great Alliance. Churchill's name would go down in history for the Grand Alliance's victories at the Battle of Blenheim in 1704 (which was utterly horrific, with over 20,000 deaths) and the Battle of Ramillies in 1706.

75. The Dutch and the English Didn't Get On

In the twenty-first century, relations between The Netherlands and the United Kingdom are very good. This was certainly not the case in the middle of the seventeenth century, with the Anglo-Dutch Wars. The Netherlands at this time was known as the United Provinces or the Dutch Republic. There was a fourth Anglo-Dutch war, but that didn't take place until the end of the eighteenth century. The Dutch during the Stuart period had a powerful, efficient navy led by competent and courageous admirals. The First Anglo-Dutch War (1652–4) was fought during the early part of Cromwell's Republic. Admiral Maarten Tromp was killed during the Battle of Scheveningen in 1653, and this was a big upset for the Dutch. General-at-Sea Robert Blake fought for the Commonweath in this war (the town of Bridgwater in Somerset is home to the Blake Museum, which is a gem for aficionados of Blake and the Stuart era).

The Second Anglo-Dutch War took place from 1665 to 1667 (never mind Charles's mistresses, this was the important stuff!). This war kicked off following the British takeover of the Dutch colony of New Amsterdam (which was then renamed New York) and the fact that the Dutch had an incredibly successful global trade network – they pretty much dominated international trade at this point. Holmes's Bonfire on 10 August 1666 saw the English sail up the Vlies estuary and set fire to over 100 Dutch merchant ships. In June of 1667, Michiel de Ruyter, one of the Dutch Republic's greatest naval admirals, led the Raid on the Medway – which resulted in a huge victory for the Dutch. They first captured the English defensive fortress at Sheerness, which was the only protective measure for the ships at port in the Medway. The Dutch set fire to six ships and sailed back home with the *Royal Charles* – England's flagship! This was a crushing blow to English morale, as the *Royal Charles* (previously named *Naseby*) was a superb first-rate ship with eighty-two guns and a capacity for 650 crew. After such a thrashing, Charles begrudgingly had to get serious about peace negotiations and the war was brought to an end with the Peace of Breda in 1667. Three years after this had been signed, Charles secretly allied himself with Louis XIV in what's known as the Secret Treaty of Dover.

What's interesting to note that despite the fact that blood ties united the nations – Charles was the uncle of the Republic's Stadtholder Prince of Orange – this wasn't enough to prevent the Third Anglo-Dutch War, which began in 1672 (the year that the Dutch call *Rampjaar*, or 'Disaster Year') and ended in 1674. This was ended with the Treaty of Westminster in 1674, which stipulated that all the islands taken by the English would be restored to the Dutch, as well as the sugarcane-rich colony of Suriname. New York, having been taken back by the Dutch, was once again in England's possession. Three years later, William III of Orange married the English princess Mary of York. Ultimately, William became King of England in 1689. Life's funny like that.

76. The Most Beautiful Women of the Late Stuart Courts Were Immortalised in Art

Beauty throughout history has been a means to power for the individuals lucky enough to possess it. This was very much the case in the Late Stuart courts. There were two series of paintings that depicted the most beautiful court ladies, and both were highly indicative of the prevailing mood of each time in which they were painted.

The first, popularly known as *The Windsor Beauties*, was painted by court portraitist Peter Lely and commissioned by the Duchess of York, Anne Hyde. Anne Hyde, the first wife of James II when he was still the Duke of York, was the mother of his two eldest daughters Mary and Anne – both of whom became queens. Anne Hyde was not known for her beauty. Indeed, many thought she was decidedly plain, and so it is interesting to note that a portrait of Anne was included in *Windsor Beauties*. There were ten 'beauties' and they were: Barbara Villiers, the Duchess of Cleveland; Elizabeth Hamilton, Countess of Grammont; Henrietta Boyle, Countess of Rochester; Minette, Madame d'Orleans; Frances Brooke, Lady Whitmore; Elizabeth Brooke, Lady Denham; Mary Bagot, Countess of Falmouth; Elizabeth Wriothesley, Countess of Northumberland; Mrs Jane Myddleton (*née* Needham); and Lady Frances Teresa Stuart. Frances was pursued ardently – and unsuccessfully – pursued by Charles II. She was distantly related to the royals, and her intoxicating beauty was so great that she was the model for Britannia.

What is striking about *The Windsor Beauties* is the

languid, sensual, even decadent aura they give off. A common criticism of these paintings is that many of the ladies depicted look the same! Lely was a very much in-demand artist, and he at his peak he was churning out one portrait after another, so it's no surprise that he was forced to standardise them.

During the reign of William and Mary, a new series of portraits of court beauties was commissioned, this time by Anne Hyde's daughter Mary, who was the lovely queen herself. Unlike Lely's *Windsor Beauties*, these *Hampton Court Beauties*, by court painter Kneller, were less overtly sensual – and this fact in itself shows the significant difference in the moral standards from King Charles II's reign and that of William and Mary. The ladies who were chosen for this series were: Frances Whitmore, Lady Middleton; Margaret Cecil, Countess of Ranelagh; Lady Mary Bentinck, Countess of Essex; Mary Scrope, Mrs Pitt; Diana de Vere, the Duchess of St Albans; Isabella Bennet, Duchess of Grafton; Carey Fraser, Countess of Peterborough; and Mary Compton, Countess of Dorset. It has often been remarked that these ladies were plainer-looking than those of the *Windsor Beauties*, and perhaps there is some truth to this. That being said, Mary wanted to select ladies not only for their beauty, but also for their virtue. Most of the *Hampton Court Beauties* are can be seen in the King's Eating Room in William III's State Apartments at Hampton Court Palace.

77. A King's Touch Was Believed to Cure Disease

For centuries, kings were believed to possess the divine power of healing. King Charles II, even though he was known for being a rational and rather sceptical man, often took part in the ceremony of 'Touching for the King's Evil'. This was a superstitious custom that maintained that if a king touched a person suffering from scrofula, that person would be cured. Scrofula is a kind of tuberculosis that affected the lymph glands.

According to some historians, the origins of this custom date back to fifth-century France and it was first started in England under King Edward the Confessor, who ruled from 1042 to 1066. Even John Flamsteed, who became the first Astronomer Royal in 1675, was a chronically ill man and was touched by King Charles II in an effort to cure him. Charles took part in many of these ceremonies because he understood the value of ritual and tradition. In 1684, *Adenochoiradelogia, or Kings-Evil-Swellings* by John Brown was published. The title is a bit of a mouthful, but this rather long work was fully devoted to the King's Evil, what it was, ways to treat it, and of course, the cure that could come from a sovereign's touch. According to this book, Charles II touched around 4,000 people a year, which brings the amount of people he touched to over 92,000.

During his Progress throughout the West Country, Charles II's eldest illegitimate son, the Duke of Monmouth, once was asked to touch a maid suffering from scrofula. He graciously obliged and she, according to the story, was cured as result. More than likely, however, this was a useful propaganda tool for those who supported Monmouth's claim to the throne, as it would prove that he was of royal blood and fit to be king. William III, who was even more sceptical than his uncle Charles, begrudgingly performed the King's Evil only on one occasion, going so far as to tell one invalid before him, 'God grant you better health and more sense.' Ouch. In the eighteenth century, Queen Anne continued this practice. One of the people she touched was two-year-old Samuel Johnson. This infant grew up to become the renowned Dr Johnson who famously compiled the *Dictionary of the English Language*, which was published in 1755. The coin, or touch piece, that she hung around Johnson's neck is now located at the British Museum in London. Queen Anne, who died in 1714, was the last British monarch to perform this ceremony.

Scrofula, or tuberculous cervical lymphadenitis, though considered quite prevalent during the Stuart period, decreased substantially during the next couple of centuries; however, it now appears to have re-emerged, following the AIDS pandemic.

78. Behn, Cavendish and Astell Were Successful Stuart-Era Female Writers

In a time when most women tended to accept their roles in society, there was a small handful of women (usually from the merchant or upper classes) who did things a little differently. Aphra Behn, who we believe may have been born in around 1640, is widely considered to be the first woman to make a living as a professional writer. She wrote several plays during the Restoration, including *Abdelazar: The Moor's Revenge* and *Oroonoko*. These plays were often set in exotic places and featured equally exotic characters, which were probably inspired by her time in Suriname. However, Behn wasn't only a playwright and poet; there is reason to believe that she may also have been a spy. She was a supporter of the Stuarts and probably held Jacobite sympathies. Unfortunately, we don't know much more about her, and she remains a truly fascinating and mysterious figure of the Restoration era. She died shortly after William and Mary came to the throne and was buried in Westminster Abbey.

Lady Margaret 'Mad Madge' Cavendish, Duchess of Newcastle-upon-Tyne, was another seventeenth century authoress. She was the wife of William Cavendish. In *The Description of a New World, Called The Blazing-World*, published in 1666, a woman finds herself in another world, reached only through the North Pole. In this work, Cavendish gave us an early kind of science fiction. She not only enjoyed writing but was also thoroughly interested in science. In the 1660s, she wrote *Observations on Experimental Philosophy* and *Grounds of Natural Philosophy*.

Mary Astell, born in 1666, brought her strongly held

views about women's roles to the literary table. Astell's *A Serious Proposal to the Ladies for the Advancement of their True and Greatest Interest, By a Lover of Her Sex* was first published in 1694. In this, she urged women to try to improve their minds and not only their physical beauty and fashion. Although she never married, she nevertheless wrote her opinions about the marital state in *Some Reflections Upon Marriage, Occasioned by the Duke and Dutchess of Mazarine's Case; Which is Also Considered*, in 1700. In this, she posed the question, 'If all Men are born free, how is it that all Women are born Slaves?' Astell also attacked male vanity in her *An Essay in Defence of the Female Sex* in 1696. Astell died in 1731.

These ladies weren't the only ones turning their hand to writing. Earlier in the Stuart era, Anglo-Welsh Katherine Philips was both a poetess and a translator of French works. She was known by the name of Orinda, and by the time of her death in 1664 she was known as 'The Matchless Orinda'. Over in France, Madame de la Fayette was anonymously publishing her works including the excellent *La Princesse de Clèves* (1678), and *La Princesse de Montpensier* (1662). In New Spain, now Mexico, Sor Juana Inés de la Cruz wrote many poems considered to be a great contribution to the literature of the Spanish Golden Age. Finally, in Italy in 1678, Elena Cornaro Piscopia became the first woman to earn a doctorate degree.

79. THE GREAT FIRE MADE A GREAT MESS

One simply cannot mention the Stuart period without mentioning the Great Plague and the Great Fire. Both major events were seen by the most devout as punishment from God. Fires were a common problem in Early Modern London. The Great Fire followed a period of exceptionally dry weather. The houses in London were notoriously tightly packed and constructed from wood. This, plus the dry weather, meant only one thing – it was the perfect setting for an inferno. On 2 September 1666, a fire broke out in a bakeshop on Pudding Lane and quickly spread to the neighbouring buildings.

Sir Thomas Bloodworth, the Lord Mayor at the time, thought it was just another fire and vulgarly replied, 'Pish! A woman might piss it out!' Not so, Mr Mayor, for the fire grew worse. There were firehooks, which were used to bring down buildings in order to stop the flames, and there were also water squirts, which would have been useful for a small fire but absolutely useless for a blazing conflagration such as this.

People began to flee, taking their families and whatever few possessions they could carry. It wasn't long before people started blaming Catholics, the French and the Dutch, and some innocent men were viciously attacked in the streets. Samuel Pepys dug a hole in his yard to bury his valuables. King Charles II, his brother James, and the Duke of Monmouth actively worked to stamp out the fire. It was feared that the fire would reach the Tower of London, where a stockpile of gunpowder was kept. Miraculously, the wind changed course and the fire died down. St Paul's Cathedral and the Royal Exchange were destroyed, along with thousands of houses and public buildings. Surprisingly, there appears to have been few deaths in the great blaze.

The aftermath of the Great Fire was a major operation. There was much to be cleared away before new construction could begin, but some people came back to start rebuilding their homes and businesses. This put a spanner in the works for people who had been working on plans, such as Sir Christopher Wren, who stepped up to offer the king his plans for reconstructing the city within a week of the inferno.

The fire may have been catastrophic, but from the ashes a new city emerged. The poet John Dryden composed the poem *Annus Mirabilis: The Year of Wonders* in 1666 and in this he wrote about the 'prodigious fire'. A 160-foot permanent Monument to the Great Fire of 1666 was designed by Christopher Wren and Robert Hooke and erected near Pudding Lane, where the fire began. This column was built between 1671 and 1677, and visitors can climb the 311 steps to the top for a nice view of the surrounding area.

80. Three Major American Universities Were Founded During the Stuart Era

In 1620, Puritans boarded the Mayflower and sailed from Southampton, England, to the New World. They may have left the Old World behind in order to start their new lives but Britain and America are still bound together by many ties, and many of those began in the Stuart era. Several universities were founded in the New World during this time. While the majority of the eight colleges referred to as 'Ivy League universities were founded in the eighteenth century, Harvard and Yale are two that were founded during the seventeenth century.

Harvard University is named after English clergyman John Harvard. Harvard, himself a graduate of the prestigious English institution of Cambridge University, emigrated to the Massachusetts Bay Colony, where he died in 1638. Robert Keayne, who was born in Windsor, England, in 1595, also emigrated to the Massachusetts Bay Colony, where he became the founder and first captain of the Ancient and Honorable Artillery Company of Massachusetts. In his will, Keayne left a substantial amount of money to Harvard College. Hugh Peter, a chaplain in the New Model Army and for Oliver Cromwell, was also instrumental in the founding of Harvard. Founded in 1636, this university has the distinction of being the oldest institution of higher education in America.

Yale University, on the other hand, was founded in the Colony of Connecticut in 1701, near the end of King William III's reign. This colony was, like the Massachusetts Bay Colony, founded by English puritans in 1638. Although it took over sixty years before the university was founded, there were some members of the colony who were interested in establishing a college back in the 1640s. The college at Saybrook was given the name 'Yale' later on during the reign of George I in 1718 in honour of Elihu Yale. This man was in the British East India Company and had travelled around the world in his profession, and he left a generous contribution to the university in his will.

In 1693, British sovereigns William III and Mary II founded the College of William & Mary in Virginia, making it the second oldest educational institution in America. The Wren Building is the oldest building at the College of William and Mary and is named after Sir Christopher Wren. Several Presidents of the United States have attended the College of William & Mary, including the third president, Thomas Jefferson. After his time as the first president, George Washington became the college Chancellor. The College of William & Mary remains a thriving and much-loved university.

81. Notorious Party-Boy Poet John Wilmot Ended Up in a Very Bad Way

His poetry was profane, his lifestyle promiscuous, his beauty angelic, and his actions reckless and debauched. John Wilmot, 2nd Earl of Rochester was, in the mere thirty-three years of his life, one of the most dissolute, wild, cocksure members of Charles II's so-called *Merry Gang*. Pepys didn't think much of him, thinking it shameful that the king could associate with 'so idle a rogue' as Wilmot. He entered the University of Oxford when he was just twelve, and it is there (as it is often said) where he fell into the world of debauchery. He wrote a poem entitled *Against Constancy*, and true to his word, although he was married to the wealthy Elizabeth Malet, he had so many mistresses and lovers that I couldn't possibly give you a number. Among these was Elizabeth Barry, one of the first actresses of the English stage. He is believed to have taken a bet to make Barry into a great actress; he coached her and she did indeed become a popular actress, also giving birth to Wilmot's daughter.

Wilmot wrote several explicit poems, including 'Signior Dildo', about, you guessed it, a dildo. His most famous lines were about King Charles II and his mistresses. 'Restless he rolls about from whore to whore, A merry monarch, scandalous and poor.' There was also an epitaph (the king was very much alive at the time): 'Here lies our Sovereign Lord the King, Whose word no man relies on, Who never said a foolish thing, Nor ever did a wise one.' Wilmot pushed the whole mockery thing a bit too far with Charles and he eventually found himself out of favour.

Bizarrely, Wilmot had a spell as a quack doctor,

taking on the guise of a 'Mrs Bendo' and giving treatments to infertile couples – and it is believed by some that he may have been the sperm-donor. Sex was a major part of Wilmot's life.

So, how did it end for this lusty libertine? Not well. You might have been wondering why he only lived until he was thirty-three, and in fact he died from a body riddled with all sorts of venereal diseases – most notably syphilis, and probably gonorrhoea. He lost his handsome looks – his nose was eaten away by syphilis and he had become blind and incontinent. His alcoholism had pickled his innards. He died on 26 July 1680, in Woodstock, Oxfordshire (this is the town right on the doorstep of Blenheim Palace, which at that time had not yet been built for the 1st Duke of Marlborough). Rochester apparently (if we can believe Gilbert Burnet, who was prone to exaggeration) had a deathbed conversion back to Christianity, and he may well have done this because he had been suffering for months due to his ailments. Who knows?

82. Stuart-Era Plays Were All the Rage

The Stuart era boasted an array of highly talented playwrights, who are well worth looking into. Across Europe, various countries experienced a 'Golden Age' of the arts, including Spain, France and England. The Elizabethan and Jacobean periods were when John Fletcher was hugely successful in his time. Not only did Fletcher rival Shakespeare, he is believed to have also collaborated with the Bard on the play *Cardenio* in 1613, which was sadly lost. Ben Jonson wrote masques and popular plays such as *Volpone, or The Foxe* (1605) and *The Alchemist* (1610). John Ford was the author of *'Tis Pity She's a Whore* and *The Broken Heart*. Plays were all the rage because anyone could go to see them at playhouses such as the Rose or the Globe.

Unfortunately, great drama came to an end once the Puritans took power during the Interregnum period under Oliver Cromwell. Readers of William Prynne's angry *Histriomastix* will understand that puritans generally believed the playhouses were obscene places that attracted whores and lewd persons and that the plays themselves had the capacity to debauch those viewing them. As a result, theatres were closed down, including the second Globe (the first was destroyed by fire in 1613). The second Globe was eventually torn down in 1644. It was a mercy that many of the great playwrights of the Elizabethan and Jacobean eras were no longer around to see this happen. By the late 1640s, Massinger, Ford, Fletcher and Jonson were all dead.

Happily for theatre-lovers, the Restoration of 1660 meant that the theatres – and playwrights – were back in business. The arts flourished once again. Restoration plays are interesting in that they could be quite explicit and controversial. William Wycherley's *The Country Wife* from 1675 was shocking for its sexual content. Sir George Etherege's *Love in a Tub* and *The Man of Mode* proved to be popular Restoration comedies. Thomas Shadwell's 1676 satire *The Virtuoso* ridiculed the experiments of the Royal Society, which proved to be a mortifying experience for some of the members. It was also during the Restoration that the first female playwright, Aphra Behn, came to prominence with plays such as the *The Rover* in 1677. Behn also wrote the 1679 play *The Feign'd Curtizans*, which she dedicated to Nell Gwynn.

In Spain, there were several notable playwrights. Lope de Vega was a prolific writer of poems and plays – his most famous being *Castigo sin Venganza* from 1631. In France, Molière, Corneille, and Racine were putting their marks upon French literature. Molière is widely considered to be one of the greatest comedic playwrights in history, and with good reason. He wrote *Tartuffe*. Jean-Baptiste Lully, Italian-born creator of some of the most extravagant French Baroque music, composed incidental music to some of these plays, most famously for Molière's *Le Bourgeois Gentilhomme*.

The plays that were created and performed during this era remain popular, especially as theatres such as the Sam Wanamaker Playhouse at the Globe usually features plays and musical events from the Stuart period.

83. James I's Daughter Elizabeth Was the 'Winter Queen'

Elizabeth Stuart was born in Scotland to King James VI/I and his queen, Anne of Denmark. Elizabeth, named after her godmother, Queen Elizabeth I, had a life full of political intrigue, beginning when she was a small child and the Gunpowder plotters were to place her on the throne when they succeeded in assassinating her father. Of course, this didn't end up happening.

In 1612, the tall, auburn-haired beauty was deemed old enough to marry, and her father decided upon the Protestant prince Frederick V Elector Palatine – a choice Elizabeth's mother strongly disapproved of. Elizabeth's beloved older brother Henry suddenly died, throwing Elizabeth and the rest of the family into grief and shock. The marriage, which had been so agreeable to Henry, finally took place on Valentine's Day the following year in 1613 (although her mother refused to attend, claiming she had an attack of gout). Happily, the political match turned into a romantic one as Frederick and Elizabeth fell in love. Their union would produce several children, including Rupert of the Rhine and Sophia, who later became the Electress of Hanover.

After they wed, Frederick took his new bride back home to Heidelberg. Religious tensions were brewing across the Holy Roman Empire and these weren't improved by the openly Catholic Ferdinand of Styra becoming King of Bohemia in 1617. During an important meeting in 1618, three men (two Catholic officials and their secretary) were thrown out of the window. The event, known as the Defenestration of Prague, was just the beginning of a series of troubles that would plague Europe – the Thirty Years War. After anguishing over the matter, Frederick decided to accept the crown of Bohemia, and the couple was given a magnificent coronation ceremony in Prague; shortly thereafter, Elizabeth gave birth to their third child, Rupert.

Their time as King and Queen of Bohemia was not to last. With the Battle of White Mountain on 8 November 1620, the Catholics once again took power. In fear of their lives, Elizabeth and Frederick left in such a hurry that baby Rupert was nearly left behind. Now in exile, Frederick and Elizabeth became mockingly referred to as the Winter King and Queen. Concerned about his sister's plight, Charles tried to obtain a marriage to the Spanish Infanta, hoping that by this he could get Spanish assistance to help Elizabeth and Frederick. It was to no avail.

In the autumn of 1632, Elizabeth's world fell apart with the death of her beloved Frederick. He had been not only her lover and companion, but also her best friend. The still-exiled widow remained in the Dutch Republic and grew fond of her eldest niece Mary, Princess Royal and Princess of Orange. Thirty years after Frederick's death, Elizabeth died on 13 February 1662, on the eve of what would have been their forty-ninth wedding anniversary. It was Elizabeth's descendants, through her daughter Sophia (sometimes referred to as the *Winter Princess*), that became the Hanoverians, or Georgians. Elizabeth's grandson, George Ludwig, became King George I and ultimately took over the rule of Britain following Queen Anne's death in 1714.

84. Puritans Really Weren't Much Fun

If you enjoy going to the theatres, dancing, and celebrating Christmas or Easter, you probably wouldn't have enjoyed living in Britain during the Republic because these things, and more, were banned. Even before the decade of the 1640s was out, puritanism had made its way to the top and several laws were passed.

In April 1644, *An Ordinance for the better observation of the Lords-Day* was passed and in this, maypoles were prohibited because they were heathenish and wicked. It also stated that copies of King Charles's *The Kings Majesties Declaration to his Subjects, concerning lawful Sports to be used* were to be burned. Why was this? Well, both James I and Charles I thought certain sports and activities were perfectly acceptable after church during the Sabbath day (Sunday), and published a *Book of Sports* to clearly list these. The puritans strongly disagreed with this because they believed it was sinful to play sports on such a day. The 1644 ordinance stipulated that wrestling, bowling, exercise, dancing, game playing and any sport (including the national favourite, football) was completely prohibited and anyone not observing this would be fined five shillings for each offence. Church organs were removed and destroyed as per May 1644's *Ordinance for the further demolishing of Idolatry and Superstition.*

Monarchists were unhappy because the new government had abolished the monarchy and had the king executed and the rest of the royal family were across the Channel in exile. Prostitution, long considered a 'necessary evil', was banned and whorehouses closed down. In 1654, horse-racing was prohibited in *An Ordinance prohibiting Horse-Races for Six Months.* Bear-baiting, cock-fighting, dog-fighting were all prohibited.

Least popular of all, Christmas was banned – but it must be said that despite the prevailing myth that states it was Cromwell's doing, it wasn't. As the Puritans gained power in England during the early Seventeenth-century, so did their distaste and abhorrence for the practice of celebrating Christ's birth with drunkenness and gluttony, and doing so on a pagan feast/festival day. On 19 December 1644, a public notice was given stating that Christmas was to be a fast day and not a day for 'carnal and sensual delights'. If you were caught roasting a Christmas turkey, you'd be in receipt of a fine. Some people simply didn't accept this, and pro-Christmas riots broke out in a few towns, but were quashed quickly. So, next time you cook up your Christmas dinner, think about how that was once prohibited.

85. Fringe Religious Groups Were Not to Be Ignored

Ever since Martin Luther's movement created a split from the Roman Catholic Church in the sixteenth century, numerous sects splintered off from this break, creating even more tumult. As more and more fringe groups began to form, each vociferously believing theirs was the true religion, they simply could not be ignored.

Arminianism was probably one of the most divisive religious movements in the early Stuart period. King Charles I quite liked Arminianism and in 1633, he controversially selected William Laud to be the Archbishop of Canterbury – a major position. Arminians had a great deal of ritual and ceremony – facts which irritated both the Anglicans (Church of England) and the more radical Puritans, who both thought Arminianism was nothing less than thinly-veiled Catholicism (that old Bogeyman). John Pym was one of the leading critics of Arminianism and he argued for the need to reform the episcopacy.

Although they weren't exactly a fringe group, the Covenanters were definitely a force to be reckoned with. The Presbyterian (Scottish Protestant) church, or the Kirk, didn't take kindly to King Charles foisting a new prayer book onto them. Everyone who was against the introduction of the prayer book signed a covenant in 1638. Now labelled the Covenanters, they played a major role in the outbreak of the civil wars.

The Fifth Monarchists were a militant Christian group who believed that they needed to overthrow the government to make way for Christ's Second Coming. This ideology came to a head in Venner's Uprising of

166,1 when Thomas Venner, a London cooper, and fifty or so men broke into St Paul's Cathedral. These Fifth Monarchists, with their manifesto, 'A Door of Hope', declared that Christ, not Charles II, was king – and one man who disagreed was shot and killed. Fights broke out on the streets and about forty people were killed in the melee. Venner and his associates were caught and condemned. Venner was subjected to the well-known hanging, drawing, and quartering. Several of the other Fifth Monarchists who were involved in the uprising were also executed – including Thomas Tonge, a relative of Israel Tonge (of Popish Plot infamy).

The Quakers, also known as the Society of Friends, were a Protestant Christian movement that was begun in the 1640s by George Fox. The Quakers believed that the sexes were equal and that slavery should be abolished – both things were considered extraordinary in the Stuart era. The most well-known seventeenth-century Quaker was one William Penn, Jr, son of Admiral William Penn. William Penn famously refused to take off his hat in front of King Charles II, and so the king light-heartedly removed his own instead. Penn gave his name to some land in the colonies – Pennsylvania, meaning 'Penn's Woods'.

Finally we have the Ranters, a group which likely existed (it's a source of debate among historians). This radical group advocated free love, and they didn't believe there was any need for ministers or even Scripture. They became so notorious that it apparently led to the Blasphemy Act of 1650 to be passed.

86. Northampton Had Its Very Own Great Fire

Northampton is a major town renowned for its shoe manufacturing, and is located in the beautiful Midlands county of Northamptonshire. This county is home to some great historic buildings including Althorp (ancestral home of the Spencer family), Holdenby House (where King Charles I was held prisoner), Fawsley Hall (where Elizabeth I once stayed) and, of course, Fotheringhay Castle (in which Mary Queen of Scots was beheaded). During the English Civil Wars, Northampton was greatly divided between those who supported Parliament and those who supported the King, but the town eventually supported the former. Northampton Castle, although it was already a ruin, was torn down even more as a kind of retribution from Charles II for siding with Parliament during the war.

It was near this castle that the Great Fire of Northampton broke out in 1675 – which had similarly devastating consequences to that of London. The fire of 1675 was by no means the town's first, for it had another major fire in 1516. This time most of the town was destroyed, leaving hundreds of families homeless. A collection was set up and the nation generously donated £25,000 (a huge sum) in order to rebuild the devastated town. All Saints' Church, which is reputed to have been designed by Sir Christopher Wren, was, according to Wren biographer Adrian Tinniswood, more likely designed by Henry Bell and Edward Edwards. This church opened in 1680. Regardless of which person actually designed it, All Saints' Church has a statue of Charles II outside above the entrance – which is always a pleasure to behold.

87. Stuart Personal Hygiene Was Not Very Hygienic

Hygiene in the Stuart age left much to be desired. Streets were mucky, covered with carcasses of dead animals and human and animal excrement. People ended up wearing pattens, wooden platform overshoes that they would slip on over their shoes. This helped to avoid getting one's feet completely covered in filth.

So what did the typical Stuart-era person do with regard to their personal hygiene? Not nearly as much as we do now! Joking aside, everyone smelt really bad, and so body odour would have been so much a fact of life that most folks would have a higher tolerance of foul smells. The diarist Samuel Pepys used to rub his body with a cloth. This could have been a cloth immersed in water and wrung out before use, but we can't know for certain. His friend John Evelyn washed his head once ... yearly! And almost nothing stopped people from all walks of life the joys of the ubiquitous parasite.

When in doubt, they masked it! The wealthier members of society were able to mask their stench with costly perfumes. Pomanders were really popular during the Early Modern period, and these were usually balls of wax mixed with lovely-smelling herbs and flowers and fixed into a small cage. This would usually hang on a cord or ribbon from a person's waist, and they could put this against their nose whenever a particularly foul smell was present.

Why didn't they simply take a bath? Some people simply thought it was not good for you to immerse the entire body in water, and anyway, if it's winter and you're freezing, with no hot water ... well, I think you get the idea. A person's hands and face were the things most likely to be cleaned daily, if possible. The early Stuart physician Thomas Cogan emphasised the importance of washing one's face, believing this to be a healthful daily act. Some people, uncomfortable with being dirty or overly pungent, would wash themselves in a river or stream. In 1654, the renowned Dutch artist Rembrandt painted *A Woman bathing in a Stream*, which shows a woman standing knee-deep in a stream. She wears only her shift, which she has pulled up to her groin as though she was going to take it off.

Although many people in the Stuart era believed that soaking in water was not good for one's health, others nevertheless did enjoy cleanliness and nice smells. Hannah Woolley, a sort of Stuart-era Nigella Lawson, advised plucking armpit hairs and then washing with a mixture of white wine and rosewater. I cannot attest as to whether this works, but surely washing the underarms at all was better than not doing so. From what relatively little information historians can gather about intimate personal ablutions, uncleanliness naturally led to disease. Presumably urinary tract infections were common, and without antibiotics, the ones that didn't clear up on their own could lead to kidney infection and death. Even in the twenty-first century, such infections are common, even though we are much more hygienic than our Stuart-era ancestors.

88. Baroque Art Was Voluptuous and Extravagant

Caravaggio, Artemisia Gentileschi, Rubens, Lely, Beale, Jordaens, Rembrandt, van Dyck, Vermeer, Velázquez. These are just some of the famous great artists who painted during the Baroque movement, which lasted from around 1600 to as late as the mid-1700s. Baroque art was often over-the-top and elaborate – the antithesis of postmodern minimalism. Baroque artwork swept through Europe in a riot of colour and movement.

Peter Paul Rubens (1577–1640), a Flemish Baroque artist, was quite possibly the most influential painter of the time and a major figure in the Counter-Reformation movement. A few of his most popular works include *Samson and Delilah* (1609–10), *Le Chapeau de Paille* (1622–5) and *The Garden of Love* (1633–4). Rubens' human figures were often very plump and this is where the term 'Rubenesque' comes from. Rubens also painted landscapes with charming bucolic scenes that undoubtedly influenced the subsequent Rococo art movement.

Cornelius Johnson (1593–1661), was an English-born painter who created some truly lovely portraits of Charles I's eldest children. Unfortunately, Johnson, for all his talent, is often overlooked in favour of his contemporary, van Dyck. Anthony van Dyck (1599–1641), another Flemish artist, was a younger contemporary of Rubens. Van Dyck is best remembered for the various equestrian portraits of his royal patron, King Charles I. In the 1630s, van Dyck painted many portraits of various members of the Caroline court. The most striking portraits of this time include *Lord John Stuart and his Brother, Lord Bernard Stuart* (*c.* 1638).

Peter Lely (1618–80) was a German-born Dutch Baroque painter who became a very in-demand portraitist during the reign of King Charles II of England. Peter Lely is best known for his series known as *The Windsor Court Beauties*, which were portraits of the great beauties of the second Charles's court. Lely is also known for his painting *Two Ladies of the Lake Family* from 1660. Lely also painted several topless portraits of Nell Gwynn and she was his model for his painting *Portrait of a Young Lady and Child as Venus and Cupid.*

Diego Rodríguez de Silva y Velázquez (1599–1660), a Spanish Baroque painter, was a court painter for the Hapsburgs in Spain. He is famed for great paintings such as *Las Meninas*, *The Surrender of Breda* and *The Rokeby Venus*. This latter painting, which was created in around 1647–50, was eventually exhibited at the National Gallery in London. In 1914, militant Suffragette Mary Richardson savagely attacked the *Venus* with a meat cleaver, causing huge damage to the priceless work of art. It was carefully restored, but even today, if you look at it up close and at a certain angle, you can still see signs of the attack.

Willem van de Velde the Elder and his son, Willem van de Velde the Younger, were two of the most important painters of Dutch marine paintings of the Baroque. Dutch influence in the art world was great at this time, for the Dutch in the seventeenth century had what's become known as the *De Gouden Eeuw* (Dutch Golden Age). This father-and-son team had their own art studio in the Queen's House in Greenwich.

89. Childbirth Was Often Fatal – to Mother and Child Alike

The prevailing mind-set of the Stuart era was that a woman needed regular intercourse for the sake of her health, which benefited from her husband's semen. Pregnancy, being the usual outcome of such activity, was a common and regular fact of life for married women in the Stuart period. Male orgasm and ejaculation was not considered sufficient to impregnate, but mutual orgasm was. Childbirth in the Stuart age (as usual throughout most of history) was often a matter of life and death, not only for the mother but the child as well. These were the days long before epidurals, before hospital births, and before proper postpartum care. Even if the baby had a normal delivery, the mother was still at risk of puerperal fever also known as childbed fever. If, however, the baby was in a difficult position, perhaps a breeched birth, this presented more problems. If thought necessary, a caesarean section would be performed.

Nicholas Culpepper's *A Directory for Midwives or A Guide for Women in their Conception, Bearing, and Suckling their Children* was published in 1651. This guide contains information on the anatomy of male and female sexual organs, gives advice on what can facilitate conception, and is largely supportive of female midwives. In contrast to Culpepper's views, William Harvey, the discoverer of blood circulation, published *De generatione animalium*, in which he opines that midwives aren't worth the trouble and women are better without them. He may have had a point, for midwives were very proactive in the birthing room. They were known use a sharp nail to break the membrane, and sometimes their interference inadvertently caused the baby's death. There was also increasing resentment from female midwives against male physicians who had been able to attend university.

Birthing chairs were constructed from wood and were adjustable and had a large opening on the seat where the baby could be passed through. In some ways, these chairs were better than the flat beds many women used to give birth in later periods. Aristocratic women would have a lying-in period. During this time, she was expected to buy items such as swaddling clothes and more linen and also to have refreshments available for the women who would come and sit with her during this time. Women further down the socioeconomic scale would usually be given aid from their local church. But having all the material comforts in the world didn't guarantee a trouble-free birth. Charles II's wife, Catherine of Braganza, had several unfortunate episodes in her quest to provide an heir to the throne.

Stillbirths and miscarriages were common. Even those who made it through the ordeal of birth weren't out of danger. Infant mortality during the Stuart era was high, and children were considered lucky if they managed to survive childhood. There were so many diseases that could kill: measles, smallpox and a whole host of diseases that could cause fever and death. Birth in the Stuart era was deadly for mother and child, but then again, it always had been.

90. The Divine Right of Kings Wasn't So Divine – It Proved Problematic

The controversial doctrine of the Divine Right of Kings held that a king had been chosen by God, and therefore was not answerable to anyone but God. A common myth surrounding this ideology is that it was something that only pertained to the Stuarts. This simply isn't the case. The belief in the Divine Right of Kings was very common throughout the ruling houses of Europe in the seventeenthcentury, and indeed before. Elizabeth I believed in the divinity of kings, which is why she found it difficult to send her cousin Mary Queen of Scots to her death. French King Henry III sent his ambassador Mauvissiére to Elizabeth to remind her that Mary was born a princess and as such was exempt from human authority. Later on in the seventeenth century, French King Louis XIV ruled very much in keeping with divine-right beliefs, even being called 'The Sun King'.

In 1598, James VII of Scotland (later James I of England) wrote *The True Law of Free Monarchies*. In this, James argued that kings became kings through the will of God, and as such were answerable to God alone and not man. Again, nothing new whatsoever from what other sovereigns in Europe believed. Logically, this meant that if a person acted against the wishes of the sovereign they were acting against the wishes of God, which was therefore sacrilege. In 1599, James followed up with *Basilikon Doron*, which was given to his son Henry and upon Henry's death, to Charles. The *Basilikon Doron* was again very supportive of the doctrine of the Divine Right of Kings, but was also a collection of advice from father to son on how to be a good king.

Charles I grew up with this belief firmly entrenched into his being. As king, he strongly believed that his will was to be accepted without question. He was gobsmacked when some in parliament didn't agree with this. He closed Parliament and began what's called his Personal Rule (also known as the Eleven Years' Tyranny). Things were fine for him for a while, until he needed money. This, combined with Charles's stubborn support of Arminianism and people such as Archbishop Laud, ultimately led to civil war and Charles's execution. His belief was the reason why Charles refused to even attempt to defend himself when he was on trial for treason. After all, a king could not commit treason.

Monarchs were not alone in believing their rule was ordained by God, for many of their subjects believed it as well. The Divine Right of Kings ideology did not end with Charles I. His sons Charles II and James II both believed in it, although Charles was less conspicuous about it than James proved to be. The Divine Right of Kings theory took another blow when James II lost his throne to William and Mary. This created an uncomfortable situation for some members of the clergy, who ended up unable to give their support to the new rulers.

91. Henry Purcell Ruled Seventeenth-Century English Baroque Music

Henry Purcell, whom we believe to have been born in 1659, remains one of the greatest of all English composers. That being said, we know surprisingly little about his personal life. Purcell was a child prodigy, able to play several instruments and compose music. He attended Westminster School and was a pupil of English Baroque composer John Blow, and was for a time a chorister and then organist at the Chapel Royal. By the age of just twenty, he was organist of Westminster Abbey. Purcell eventually found a royal patron in King Charles II, under whom he wrote many works.

The range of his musical composition was impressive. Purcell had the ability to convey the depths of tragedy ('When I am Laid in Earth' from *Dido and Aeneas*) to the comical ('I'm drunk' from *The Fairy Queen*). *The Fairy Queen* was based on William Shakespeare's comedy *A Midsummer Night's Dream*. *Dido and Aeneas* was an important work of English Baroque opera. Purcell also wrote secular music, sacred music, and all to a very high standard. He wrote incidental music for nearly fifty plays, including Aphra Behn's *Abdelazer: Or The Moor's Revenge*, for which he wrote the unforgettable *Rondeau,* famously used in the television series *The First Churchills*.

When James II came to power, Purcell appears to have taken a slight dive in popularity with the new king. Purcell was a Protestant, and the king was increasingly favouring Catholics in his reign. His popularity was once again in the ascendant when William and Mary came to the throne in 1689. In Queen Mary II, Purcell found a much more enthusiastic patroness. He wrote several birthday odes for Queen Mary II including, *Love's Goddess sure was Blind*. In 1692, he wrote *An Ode for St. Cecilia's Day*, which was very popular. Arguably his greatest achievement, the *Funeral Music for Queen Mary II* – which was performed at her funeral in March of 1695 – has all the elements that would later make Mozart's *Requiem* so brilliant: stateliness, a haunting poignancy and unforgettable melodies.

The Indian Queen proved to be Purcell's last and unfinished semi-opera, and was completed by his younger brother, another talented composer, Daniel Purcell. For some years tuberculosis was considered the probable cause, but Purcell's biographer Maureen Duffy suggests influenza, which in turn led to bronchitis or pneumonia. We may never know exactly what led to his death in 1695, but there were various rumours, including a popular but probably apocryphal story that he came home late on a rainy night only to find that his wife, Frances, had locked him out of the house.

Purcell was buried in Westminster Abbey, where a fittingly elaborate monument was erected to mark his grave. Across the street from New Scotland Yard in London stands a modern art sculpture dedicated to Purcell and entitled *The Flowering of the Baroque Mind*. Purcell's story also found its way onto the screen in the film *England, My England*.

92. The Great Plague Was Pretty Nasty

Plague is one of the most lethal diseases in human history. Symptoms of plague include fever, buboes (painful swellings of the lymph nodes), vomiting and finally death – and all this takes either between three to five days or up to two weeks. It is generally believed that there were three variants of the plague. The Bubonic plague, as mentioned before, was most common during this outbreak; next was the pneumonic plague, which would attack the lungs and was almost certainly fatal; and finally, septicaemic plague, which went into the bloodstream and could quickly become deadly. The plague epidemic that swept through London in 1665 was the worst outbreak the city had faced since the Black Death of 1348. Plague spread from fleas on rats (although new research suggests that gerbils may have been the original carriers), and these would carry the bacterium *Yersinia pestis*. Plague had been an intermittent problem throughout the Stuart age, cropping up from time to time, but this was different.

The Turks and the Dutch had already had bad outbreaks of plague earlier in the 1660s, and with the increase in trading routes, it's no surprise that the disease turned up in Britain. In London, the insalubrious slums of St Giles-in-the-Fields were the first place where the dreadful contagion began to show up. Those who could leave London did; the royal court moved out of the city. Queen Catherine and her ladies travelled to Tunbridge. Infected houses were marked with a red cross on the door, and the words 'God have mercy on us' would also be placed here. Sick persons were taken to the pest houses. On Monday 26 June, 1665, Pepys wrote in his Diary that 'the plague increases mightily', followed the next day by 'in my way to Westminster Hall, I observed several plague houses in King's street'.

The common belief at this time was that plague was spread by foul smells, and so to counteract this, fumigation was considered the best deterrent. Fumigation involved burning strong-smelling things such as brimstone, amber and saltpetre. Those who were plague doctors wore beak-shaped masks and the beak would be filled with sweet-smelling herbs – again, with the belief that this would prevent contagion. With this idea in mind, many people (including children) took up smoking tobacco, believing again that this would halt the disease from entering their lungs. Fumigation and smoking weren't the only preventative measures that were used, for stray dogs and cats were slaughtered as well.

While the mortality rate was pretty bad, not everyone who contracted the plague died. Prince Rupert's younger brother Maurice contracted it during the English Civil War and survived. Some even survived in the pest houses and were given a certificate that they were cleared of the plague. At its peak, 7,000 people died from the plague each week. It is estimated that over 100,000 people may have died from this episode of plague. The Great Fire of London ultimately destroyed the foul dwellings that had been so perfect for the spreading of disease in 1666.

93. Sir John Vanbrugh Wrote Naughty Plays and Designed Stately Buildings

Sir John Vanbrugh was born in 1664 and was, like many of his contemporaries, a man who was very good at several things. As part of the generation who grew up under the wing of Sir Christopher Wren, Vanbrugh learned from some of the best architects of his age. He often collaborated with Nicholas Hawksmoor on various architectural designs. Together, they designed Castle Howard, Blenheim Palace and the Orangery at Kensington Palace. It was during his time as the main architect of Blenheim Palace that he quit the job because of Lady Marlborough's overbearing and dictatorial manner. Hawksmoor had to continue where Vanbrugh left off.

Architecture was just one of Vanbrugh's pursuits. He loved the theatre and was both a playwright and theatre manager – most notably of the Queen's Theatre in Haymarket, London. Although this theatre burnt down in the eighteenth century, Her Majesty's Theatre (where Andrew Lloyd Webber's *Phantom of the Opera* has been since 1986) has been on the site since 1897. Vanbrugh's plays were reputed to be rather naughty and created a good deal of controversy because of their explicit sexuality. In 1696, he wrote *The Relapse*, which is about a reformed rake, Loveless, who despite being married to Amanda suffers a relapse when he falls for Berinthia. In 1697, his play *The Provoked Wife* provoked a stir, as the comedy was about a lady in an abusive relationship.

He was also a political man, having been supportive of the Glorious Revolution in the late 1680s. He spent some time in the Bastille prison in Paris on a charge of espionage. Vanbrugh was also a member of the Kit-Kat Club (a Whig-heavy early-eighteenth-century drinking club), and the most popular portrait of him is from a series of portraits that Sir Godfrey Kneller painted of the club's members. This striking portrait, with Vanbrugh in his prime, now hangs in the National Portrait Gallery in London.

94. 'Colonel' Blood Nearly Stole the Crown Jewels … and Was Ultimately Rewarded

In 1671 the Crown Jewels were nearly stolen. Self-styled 'Colonel' Thomas Blood's daring attempt to steal the Crown Jewels is one of the most often-told facts about the Stuart era. Blood struck up a friendship with the Keeper of the Jewels and on 9 May, he and several other men visited the Tower. They beat the Keeper hard on the head, gagged and bound him before turning their attentions to what they'd come for. They bashed down the crown, and the orb and sawed the sceptre in half, then hid these precious items among their clothing. It just so happened that the Keeper's son arrived in time to see what was going on and a chase ensued, but the villains were apprehended. This hadn't even been Blood's first crime. Back in 1663, the former Irish Parliamentarian had attempted to take control of Dublin Castle, but was thwarted and was forced to flee in order to save his life. He also tried to kidnap the Duke of Ormond on a couple of occasions.

Blood went back to the Tower – this time as prisoner – but he managed to get an audience with the king, who visited him in his cell. Whatever was spoken in that private interview worked out in Blood's favour. King Charles II, instead of severely punishing Blood for his crime, ended up giving him a reward – lands in England and Ireland. On 1 August 1671, Charles's Secretary of State, Lord Arlington, noted that Thomas Blood had been given a pardon from any and all crimes from 1660 to that point. Why did Charles do this? I don't believe anyone's been able to figure that out.

The coronation regalia Blood tried to steal were

actually quite new. During the Commonwealth, Parliament decided to do away with all vestiges of monarchy. Cromwell ordered all of the royal regalia to be burned and melted down, and so it was done. Only a few items were smuggled away in time and preserved, including a coronation spoon. Most of the Crown Jewels we can see in the Jewel House at the Tower of London today were made for Charles II in 1661 for his coronation. Other items are from subsequent monarchs.

95. Many of Charles I's Regicides Met Ghastly Ends

A regicide is the act of killing a king, and the word is also given to a person who takes part in the killing of a king. At the Restoration of the monarchy in 1660, the executed king's son – now Charles II – understandably wanted revenge for his father's murder. This topic, about the fates that befell those men who had signed Charles I's death warrant in 1649, has been the subject of several books, most notably Don Jordan and Michael Walsh's *The King's Revenge* and Charles Spencer's *Killers of the King*. Some regicides fled abroad to Europe, some to the colonies in the New World (the Americas). Others stayed put, and were subjected to some cringe-worthy executions.

Regicide was tantamount to treason, and the punishment for treason was 'hanging, drawing and quartering' (though it must be said, that saying is literally out of order – traitors were *drawn* in a sledge first, then *hanged* until they passed out, cut down from there and revived in time to feel their intestines removed and burned in front of them. Their genitals would be cut off, followed by their head, and then their body was *quartered*).

In the pamphlet *The Speeches and Prayers of Some of the Late King's Judges*, published in 1660, the purported last speeches of the following ten men were documented: Major-General Thomas Harrison, John Carew, Justice Cooke, Hugh Peters, Thomas Scott, Gregory Clement, Colonel Adrian Scrope, Colonel John Jones, Colonel Daniel Axtell, and Colonel Francis Hacker. Harrison was of the radical Fifth Monarchists and he was one of the first to receive the penalty for treason.

Others fled, but that didn't save them. Lord de Lisle, one of the king's judges, was killed at Lausanne about twenty miles from Geneva. According to a letter located in *State Papers, Geneva* at the UK National Archives, two mysterious men one day appeared in a small village. Then, near the entrance of a church one of these men shot Lisle dead as he made his way to attend church. The two men fled as quickly and stealthily as they had come. William Goffe, John Dixwell, and Edward Whalley all fled across the Atlantic to the colonies there, where they lived the rest of their lives in hiding.

What about those who had died before the Restoration? Death was no deterrent for the king's vengeance. Cromwell, who had been so gleeful when he signed the king's death warrant, had died in 1658 and was buried in Westminster Abbey. Charles II had him disinterred and subjected Cromwell's corpse to a posthumous traitor's execution. The same fate also befell Cromwell's son-in-law Henry Ireton – his corpse was also exhumed. John Bradshaw, another regicide who had been buried in Westminster Abbey, was disinterred upon Charles II's orders as well. All three had their heads mounted on spikes outside Westminster Hall – the place where they signed for the death of their king all those years before. But Charles II, in spite of this vengeance, was not a bloodthirsty man and he soon tired of all the death.

96. Hooke Showed Us Another World with His Microscope

Microscopy is a study of objects with the use of a microscope. This means that you can have a look at blood, urine, a sliver of potato, and you'll see some amazing (and some creepy) things. Both the word microscopy and what it entails first came about during the Stuart era, around 1660 or so. In the Dutch Republic (the present-day Netherlands), Anton van Leeuwenhoek made some great advances in the field of microscopy. Not only did he greatly improve microscope functionality, but some of the things he studied under his microscope included bacteria and even his own semen (when he observed spermatozoa, he concluded that each sperm contained a mini person, which goes along with Preformationism – a popular theory during the Stuart era). Although van Leeuwenhoek is often called 'The Father of Microscopy', he wasn't the only one observing and researching with the aid of a microscope.

Over in England, Robert Hooke made major strides in microscopy. Hooke has had the misfortune of being one of those figures who gets neglected a lot and there's no justification for that. He was a brilliant scientist who discovered the theory of elasticity (Hooke's Law) and was the inventor of a variety of scientific instruments. Throughout the 1660s and 70s, he was the Curator of Experiments at the Royal Society and then Professor of Geometry at Gresham College.

But it was his ground-breaking and bestselling 1665 book, *Micrographia: Or Some Physiological Descriptions of Minute Bodies, Made By Magnifying Glasses; With Observations and Inquiries thereupon,* which made Hooke great. In *Micrographia*, Hooke discovered and coined the term *cell* – which those of us who studied biology at school remember to be the smallest or most basic unit of life. The illustrations in *Micrographia* are some of the most famous scientific drawings ever, let alone from the seventeenth century, the most recognisable being the drawing of a flea, with the various parts of its body labelled. Hooke also examined his urine under the lens of his microscope and found,gravel', which when magnified looked rather a lot like jewels. He also had a look at things such as a stinging nettle leaf and the illustration for this clearly shows all the thorny bits. Hooke and all those who worked in microscopy showed that there was a whole new world to explore – found with a microscope.

Hooke was a good friend of Christopher Wren and the pair often collaborated in both scientific and architectural pursuits. Unfortunately, Hooke was not without rivals. It has long been suggested that Isaac Newton played a major role in Hooke's legacy because they had had hostile interactions with each other. Figuratively speaking, it's a crime that so few people know about Hooke. But you do now, so that's a start!

97. Celia Fiennes Was a Stuart-Era Female Travel Expert

Celia Fiennes was an independent-spirited aristocratic lady who was born in Wiltshire in 1662, during the Restoration. Fiennes is important because she travelled extensively throughout England between 1682–1712, noting her thoughts as she went along. The most surprising element of her travels is that she was neither married nor escorted properly for the time (she usually only had servants with her). In her writings, Fiennes describes her travels to English towns and cities such as Bath, Yeovil and Daventry, among others. She visited several stately homes (including Woburn Abbey) and palaces, including her visit to Hampton Court Palace, where she had a look around Queen Mary II's temporary apartments in the old Tudor Water Gallery. She also explored northern areas such as Preston, Manchester, Durham, and the beautiful Lake District. Fiennes described in detail the appearances of the areas and houses she saw, and even commented that Hyde Park was 'green and full of deer, there are large ponds with fish and fowle'.

Fiennes was even a spectator during the funeral of Queen Mary II in 1695, and she described the ceremony in detail. Nowadays, Celia Fiennes is best known for her travel memoirs, which were finally published in the nineteenth and twentieth centuries: *Through England on a Side Saddle*, and now *The Journeys of Celia Fiennes*. In these writings, which she wrote solely for her family, she described her remarkable journeys on horseback throughout England. Although these writings were meant for her family only and never published during her lifetime, the wealth of information contained in them was too great to be kept hidden.

98. Ashmole and Bodley Left Us a Museum and a Library

The great Ashmolean Museum and the Bodleian Library at the University of Oxford are two of the most renowned institutions in the world, and both were founded in the Stuart era. Sir Thomas Bodley was a courtier during the reign of the last Tudor monarch, Elizabeth, and when he retired from all that he put all his efforts into founding a library (which opened in 1602). This wasn't the first library at the university, for back in the fifteenth century, Humphrey of Lancaster, 1st Duke of Gloucester, donated a couple of hundred books. Sadly, during the English Reformation many books and furniture were removed. The oldest reading room at the current Bodleian is called Duke Humphrey's Library after the duke. Sir Thomas Bodley died on 28 January 1613, but his great library has been very useful for scholarly research ever since.

The Ashmolean Museum boasts a great assortment of objects from throughout history. There are items from the Stuart age, including musical instruments (including a Stradivarius *guitar*), earthenware bowls and a large selection of paintings including an incredible collection of seventeenth century Dutch still-lifes. Even gloves belonging to Queen Anne when she was Princess of Denmark are on display (Anne attended the museum's opening on 21 May 1683). The creator of this magnificent museum was the great English antiquarian Elias Ashmole (1619–92). His own collections were substantially increased with the addition of John Tradescant's collection of curiosities (Tradescant was Ashmole's friend).

Ashmole was more than a collector of strange and

wonderful objects: he was also a politician. If his belief that spiders would ward off the plague is anything to go by, Ashmole was rather superstitious. Ashmole was also a Freemason. Like many gentlemen of his class, he had interests in alchemy and science. In keeping with these interests, he was the author of several works, including *Theatrum Chemicum Brittannicum*, *The Glory of Light* and *The Antiquities of Berkshire*. Ashmole died in 1692.

99. A Royal Birth Started a Revolution

When King James II's wife Mary of Modena gave birth to a son in the summer of 1688, it sent in motion events that culminated in the Glorious Revolution. Almost immediately after James Francis Edward Stuart's birth, rumours circulated that the boy was a changeling who had been smuggled into the delivery room in a warming pan. The false story continued that the queen had given birth to a stillborn child and this other newborn was put in its place. This silly rumour stuck and the child maliciously became known as the 'warming-pan baby'.

King James II was already rather unpopular by the time he ascended the throne in early 1685 following the death of his brother, King Charles II. James, whom some had nicknamed 'Dismal Jimmy', lacked many of the personable qualities that had made Charles popular. James was, by contrast, without a sense of humour and staunchly Catholic in a time in which many were openly hostile to Catholicism. Once upon the throne, he soon had to deal with a rebellion – led by his eldest nephew, the Duke of Monmouth – and although the rebellion was stamped out quickly, the brutality of the punishments impacted further upon the king's increasingly negative reputation.

During his reign he had dissenting bishops put on trial and gave major government positions to Catholics – all of this added further to his unpopularity. Just over the English Channel, the autocratic Catholic Louis XIV had revoked the Edict of Nantes and issued the Edict of Fontainebleau. French Protestants, the Huguenots, were in effect told that they had to convert to Catholicism or face fines or worse. These were the *dragonnades*, and thousands of Huguenots fled into more religiously tolerant countries, such as the Dutch Republic and England. The fear was that James would pull a move similar to his French cousin or, worse, that he might continue where Mary I – 'Bloody Mary' – had left off, and begin a systematic persecution of Protestants in England, Scotland, and Ireland.

Although James and Mary of Modena had had sons before, they had all died and his heir remained his daughter from his first marriage (to Anne Hyde), Mary, Princess of Orange. The baby boy's birth not only meant that Mary was no longer next in line for the throne, but that a Catholic succession was assured. This situation proved to be the straw that broke the camel's back. Mary, crucially, had been brought up in the Anglican Church and was a popular heir, especially as she had married her first cousin and hero of Protestant Europe, William of Orange.

When Mary chose to support her husband over her father, her decision changed the course of the British monarchy. William and Mary were, in effect, constitutional monarchs, and with their agreement to the Bill of Rights (which gave more power to Parliament, thus decreasing royal power) the beginning of constitutional monarchy began. Mary's new baby brother would never inherit his throne and would become known as 'The Old Pretender', and his son, after him, 'The Young Pretender'.

100. Stuart Misfortunes Led to Hanoverian Power

Following the Restoration in 1660, there was a great hope that with the return of the king there would be continued peace throughout the land and a secured, Protestant succession. Unfortunately, things did not work out that way, and Charles II (as we have already learned) was very good at impregnating his numerous lovers. Sadly, although he did get his wife Catherine of Braganza pregnant, she had a great deal of trouble conceiving and was ultimately unable to provide an heir. After Charles's death, James II came to the throne. Ironically, although they were also plagued by a series of misfortunes, he and his wife Mary of Modena eventually did have a healthy son and heir, who because of his parents' Catholicism, was cut off from his birthright.

James's daughters, Mary and Anne, who came to the throne after his exile, did not fare as well. Anne, though blessed with a loving and stable marriage to Prince George of Denmark, had one of the most tragic gynaecological histories of any monarch in British history. In 1684, the then-Princess Anne married George of Denmark and quickly became pregnant – beginning a long and painful series of miscarriages, stillbirths and infant deaths. Smallpox, which Anne had had before in 1677, came to her door again. There is reason to suggest that in March of 1695, Anne may have also suffered from a phantom pregnancy, or *pseudocyesis*, a condition in which a woman believes she is pregnant. This is something that Frederick Holmes, in his book *The Sickly Stuarts*, suggests probably affected her elder sister, Mary, as well. William and Mary, who had

been married since 1677, were plagued by at least two miscarriages and died childless. Mary, as Princess of Orange, was expected to provide an heir; this intense psychological desire may have caused her to have symptoms akin to those associated with pregnancy.

By the end of 1700, Anne's only surviving son, William Henry, Duke of Gloucester, was dead at the age of eleven. And so, despite Anne having had between sixteen and eighteen pregnancies (there is some debate as to the actual number), none of her children survived. The resulting Act of Settlement in 1701 meant that anyone who professed to be a Catholic would be automatically excluded from the line of succession.

As a result, a great many people who were more closely linked to throne by blood were excluded in favour of the Hanoverians. The reason for this was quite simple. Electress Sophia of Hanover (sister of Rupert of the Rhine) was the daughter of Stuart Princess Elizabeth, who was in turn the daughter of King James I. As this line was predominantly Protestant, they became the heirs to the Protestant Stuarts' throne. And thus, an indirect Stuart descendent still sits on the throne to this day.